TWENTY-TWO MONTHS UNDER FIRE

Henry Page Croft

www.General-Books.net

Publication Data:

Title: Twenty-Two Months Under Fire
Author: Croft, Henry Page, 1881-1947
Publisher: London : J. Murray
Publication date: 1917
Subjects: World War, 1914-1918

TWENTY-TWO MONTHS UNDER FIRE

INTRODUCTION

War is one of those things the British people for nearly half a century have refused to contemplate, and the mere fact that the seas encircled the British Isles was sufficient to lull our people into a dreamland in which we pretended that a world war was impossible. War is an exacting thing: it demands great effort, it imperils wealth, it threatens luxury, it interferes with the sports and pleasures of the peopleâ in a word, the idea of war was unpopular, and because it was unpopular, those who seek the favour of the British people and guide them avoided all mention of the ugly thing.

Preparation for war meant taxation, and how could any rising statesman, or still less any political party, advocate taxation when the fight for success in the political arena depended upon which section could promise most individual gain to the individual elector?

So it was that we drove war from the ambit of our thoughts, we of the British race who have the greatest frontiers of the world to defend, and from whom the world has most to gain.

All parties ignored the overwhelming evidence which hit us in the face from Germany. No party would listen to Lord Roberts and none was found to defend that great man from the taunts and gibes of second-rate political adventurers.

An annual expenditure on a national army of five days' cost of this war would have probably given us peace and most certainly would have saved Belgium, and deprived our enemies of that great start which they gained whilst our patriotic people, untaught, unorganised, unarmed, began to learn the business of war.

The greatest Empire the world has ever known at the striking of the decisive hour of fate could only place four divisions in the decisive theatre of warâ that was the prepared effort of 400,000,000 subjects of our King.

This is not the hour to apportion the blame, neither is it the moment to ask how it was that the guardians of this great heritage had failed, with such criminal neglect, to organise the Empire and to prepare for its defence. The time will come when these questions will be asked with some persistence, then countless widows and orphans will demand an account of the stewardship which deceived and fooled the people, and finally plunged a nation into a war which was known to be imminent and for which no sort of preparation was made.

One fact stands out with a clearness that must be obvious, and that is, that the present political system of the British Empire has failed, and never again can issues of peace and war, or the defence of the Empire, be left in the hands of men whose sole obsession is political popularity, and who were so greatly occupied with party strife that they gambled with and risked the life of the greatestâ yes, still the greatest nation on earth.

To the men of Oversea Dominions, whom I have lived with, fought alongside of, and learnt to admire on the field of battle, even more than in the days when I endeavoured humbly to serve the Imperial ideal at home, I would add this request: Do not judge our people by our political rulers, but rather join with the people of the old country to purify a system which is at fault, for whilst our politicians have failed, those also in the younger countries were little more successful in teaching the true path of patriotismâ that freedom is of more worth than wealth.

We have learned together how to fight, and the blood of our dead is soaking the soil which they together have made immortal; let us now start out to design and build a palace on foundations of such depth and thickness that it shall stand for ever, but to secure this end, let us tolerate no half measures in the great memorial to our fallen. We have been up against hell for a common ideal, and whilst in the years to come each of our countries will work out as heretofore its own destiny, in those great matters which vitally concern us all and affect our common fate, let us come together in a complete, imperishable partnership.

This war has found the nations of the British standing together, fighting together, dying together, and is not the great lesson which it teaches and which the ages can never dim, first, that scattered as we are we can still claim similar qualities of steadfastness of purpose, courage against all odds, greatness in adversity, and liumility in our hours of victory, and second that severally we could not have lasted the course, but together we shall win through? The states of the Empire are essential one to the other, and henceforth we who have all to gain by the handclasp of fraternity will do well to enter a commonwealth in which we shall find our League of Peace, a commonwealth of all the British states.

In the hope and belief that out of the blinding dust and shattered wreckage of this war will come so great a good, I dedicate this little book of impressions to my comrades of the battlefield.

PART I THE TERRITORIALS

We were a subject of amusement to civilians and tolerated by regulars as an inferior article which probably meant well, but we continued in our spare hours to try and fit ourselves for the coming of " the Day." It occurred to us that the German nation was a practical one, and that if the day was not coming they would hardly squander the fruits of an amazing economic success in building a vast Navy and in increasing what was already the most complete military machine in the world. Further, if the Germans did not mean business why was the whole of their people ready to imbibe the doctrines of Bernhardi, and why did the countless writings of similar description find such a ready market amongst all classes of Germans; why was the German Navy League encouraged to give lantern lectures to every school in Germany; why was the final slide for the German youth always a picture of the sinking of the British fleet by that of Germany?

The evidence was too strong, and so in the regiment to which I had the honour to belong we believed in the German peril, and in spite of laughter and taunts we decided to fit ourselves for the day.

Three years before war was declared the 1st Battalion of the Hertfordshire Regiment was reported on as " fit for active service," and so we could afford to smile at those who asked us why we wasted our precious holidays in trainingâ had not the regular soldiers themselves declared us worthy to fight with them when war came?

The annual camp was taking place at Ashridge Park, Berkhampstead, and our training proceeded whilst some of us wondered about Europe.

The " Terriers " were playing at soldiei-s, and suddenly the Austrian ultimatum was sent and we knew our play was not in vain. We quickened our efforts; war burst on our country; our camp was broken up; and we realised we were to pay the proud penalty of patriotism.

We were business men, tradesmen, work- ing men, each concerned in the profession or job which we had made our hfe's affair, and when the call came we had to break with our life's workâ no time for us to settle our business, no time to find substitutes, our house was left in disorder, and we marched towards the east coast. Some day, when England has time to think, she will thank her Territorials, who had to make far the biggest sacrifice, and she will realise that without the " peace time patriot" the " regular Army" could not have left her shores, and she will remember that whilst the new armies were learning to form fours without rifles or uniform, which little details our thoughtful Government had forgotten to provide, the Territorial units which had made good were already proceeding to Belgium to fill the shattered gaps of the immortal British Army.

We counted it a misfortune that we were part of the East Anglian Division, because it seemed that our very name would kccp us hugging the vulnerable shores of England, perhaps till the end of all things, so we settled down with no little restlessness to training in the eastern counties; but we had forgotten the great general who had declared us fit for war, and on November 2nd, 1914, we got our orders for the front. The Hertfordshire Regiment became very unpopular with the rest of the division, for had we not been chosen to go to the centre of the world whilst all the other battalions stayed behind?

It was in the early hours of the morning, the sleepy Suffolk town was still more sleepy than usual as we said good-bye to our women, and were assured by them that of course we were only going to defend the lines of communication. Oh yes, we said, of course it means the lines of communication I Quietly in the early morning we fell in by companies and then marched for the station with mighty song, whilst nightcaps and other unusual garments appeared in the windows as we sang our way to the train.

Our comrades of the brigade sent a band to play the train offâ to play the " lucky devils " away to the place where men meet men. " See you soon," said the men of the rest of the brigade! Little we thought that within a year so many of the rest of the brigade would perish in Gauipoh, when they too became " lucky devils." So long, see you soon!

Southampton; packed like flies in a ship equipped for artilleryâ a hard bed this, and how we used to groan at a straw bed in a splendid farm barn! Havreâ yes, there it is, full of transports. Hospital ships, ugh! A weary wait as the transport is disembarked. A regiment of yeomanry marches pastâ " good old Territorials! "â and now we are off on French soil for the camp.

Crowds of French civilians line the streets of Havre, fluttering handkerchiefs, friendly smiles, " etes vous les Gardes?"â Yes, the Herts Guardsâ great laughter and much singing, pretty faces in the upper windows. We begin to talk Frenchâ such French! and we have a comfortable feeling that now we have arrived France is saved.

The rest campâ oh yes, we shall probably be here for a fortnight; but what a camp! depressing, " not 'arf "; let's be getting on 1 Short route march next day; we shall probably do this every day, nobody knows how long.

Splendid dinner in a restaurant this second night in France. But who is this disturbing the coffee? An orderly, with orders to move at 3 a. m.: five hours to get back to the battahon, sleep and strike camp. The authorities seem to be in a great hurry.

A weird march in the early morning pitch dark, arrival at the station; wait here for orders, so the whole battalion lies down on the cobbles. Dawn comes, and parties of men of many British regiments steal by from the station. Tired men, weary men, ragged men, men who have been " there," and who are recovering from slight ailments and soon to return.

The train at lastâ all aboard for no one knows where. How long the journey is, how slowly the train moves! The second morning early we arrive at St. Omer.

There is much speculation as to our duties. Some say that we shall form the bodyguard of the Commander-in-Chief; some say we shall stay here in reserve.

We march to our first French village to get acclimatisedâ the hint is given us that we shall be here some time, probably a fortnight; we also learn that tlie attacks on the British line at Ypres have been terrific. We do some field work and drill, and we can hear the guns quite plainly.

The Commander-in-Chief was here this morning. He only saw one company, but he said nice things to be conveyed to all of us. We come to the conclusion we are splendid fellows!

We are to do an attack practice before staff officers from St. Omer; all goes well, the attack practice is carried out just according to book. The staff officers express surpriseâ why should they express surprise! Next day off to dig; probably we shall dig every day for a fortnight. Yes, that is what we are here for. We site the trench with field of fire in places fifty yards. Oh yes, " capital field of fire," says the expert; but say we, this isn't the book. Never mind, you've got fifty yards. Yes, we must hit 'em at fifty yards.

Dig away, come on, you must get down; don't mind how tired you get, show these regulars what we can do! We are really getting quite tiredâ what's this? Orders to move at once to join the 4th Guards Brigade at Ypresâ quite right too; Herts Guards to the Guards Brigade; but what fools we were to dig so hard, and there is a six-mile march back to billets.

Buses; rows of busesâ Marble Arch, Putneyâ half an hour to pack upâ got to start at once. Load up outside and inside. Quite amusing at first this journey, but as the hours slipped by more and more fatiguing.

The road is full of interest. British and French cavalry, gunners and infantry in small parties, a stream of Red Cross carsâ these latter seemed never to endâ and then the rain descended and half the battalion for hours had to endure a soaking in the dark as the buses skidded this side and that; and then still more Red Cross cars, and one began to realise that we were nearing the edge of things.

All my life the persistent theory had held my mind that if ever I went into action I should run away the instant I came under fire, and now this fateful experience seemed to be imminent. The hours in that bus were spent in thought, with little consolation; and the weariness of the journey, coupled with the discomfort of those outside in the wet, tended to expel even excitement, and so the recurring question, "How shall I behave under fire? " I expect many have asked themselves this same question, perhaps with equally unsatisfactory results. I turned to history, and wondered how my forbears felt on similar occasions, and I remembered one, a bishop, who whilst the soldiers of Cromwell tried to stop him preacliing in Hereford Cathedral, calmly finished his sermonâ which was on sacrilegeâ whilst the soldiers kept their muskets aimed at his head. I nov came to the conclusion if I had been in the pulpit, I should on the appearance of the soldiers have speedily pronounced the blessing and let the congregation disperse.

At last, about midnight, we pulled up in Vlamertinghe and " debussed," if that is the right expression, into a dreary street, whilst the rain came down in torrents and rations were served outâ a tiresome business at any time, especially so when the food was all packed on the last bus (which did not arrive for an hour after the head of the column), and had to be issued in pitch dark whilst all ranks were soaked through.

One had time to look around, and here again, whilst we waited, a very large number of French Red Cross wagons kcpt passing.

whilst the sky was bright with the flash of the guns and we had our first education in the music of artillery.

After waiting some time, a staff officer came up and uttered the cheery words, "You will go to a farm to-night," and we all thought of nice barns, straw, and coffee, etc. Things were very lively, he told us; " they have made a big effort to smash us, and to-day their attack has been on a very big scale, but we have held them. I think we will take the long road; they have been shelling both heavily to-day, but the long road least." Oh yes, "How nice!" we said.

Near midnight we were ready to march, and conducted by our guide we set off on the road to Ypres. The rain ceased, and we entered the ancient city under a bright moon. The stricken town was very silent, although in the distance we could hear the incessant artillery duel. Sometimes we had to go slow, owing to the ruins of a house being scattered over the road; here we saw houses still burning after the day's bombardment, then a body huddled in a corner, and we knew that this was war.

On we marched until suddenly the grand old building of the Cloth Hall loomed up bffore us in all its beauty, that edifice which within a week was to fall, shattered by the unsparing guns of the enemy; and so on we went when suddenly, what was that?

Swishâ crash! a blinding flash all round the head of the battalion, and before we had recovered from our surprise, again swish-crash, this time all in one; and as tiles and bricks fell round us I found myself knocked on my knees with a dull thud on my back. For a moment the head of my company was scattered over the road, but only for a moment. " Any one hit? " Nothing serious, only half a dozen bruises, " lead on." Now shrapnel was freely bursting over the centre and rear of the battalion, and we marched on through the zone, and we in front began wondering how many casualties behind. So this is war. When will my turn come? Will it be to-night, tomorrow, or next week? Somehow I hoped it might be a week!

On we marched, ever nearer the inferno, and now the roll of rifle fire was incessant, and the high ground of Zonnebeke and Zillebeke was continually lit up by gun-flash and bursting shrapnel. Tlie men were very tired, for, remember, we had been early afoot digging at St. Omer that day, and had marched twelve miles before we ever took our trip on the bus to this happy land.

Halt! A chateau, the divisional headquarters of Sir Charles Munro. Fresh guides, and on again to our cosy farm! Arrived at last; three companies will go into the rest trenches, and one in the farm. Rest trenches indeed, as we stumbled through the dark and sorted ourselves out in a maze of glorified ditchesâ oh the lucky beggars in the farm!

Mount sentries. Where are we, where are the enemy, where is our firing line? God only knows! and so to sleep on the sodden mud, which was oozing from hours of rain.

Early awake, those who had slept through the artillery row, and shivering with cold, we started to munch biscuits, and a few more adventurous spirits managed to kindle little fires to cook a hot drink, and so our first morning in Armageddon hailed usâ the morning of November 12th, 1914.

We reasoned amongst ourselves that of course they will rest us to-day after our exacting experiences of yesterday, but " they " are unreasonable people evidently, because we had hardly begun to accustom ourselves to the enjoyment of life in a muddy field when suddenly a staff officer galloped up and in a very unemotional voice, speaking very slowly, told us that the French had been driven in on our left and that we were to go up behind them and dig a new line.

We decided to cultivate unemotional ways, and in unemotional voices ordered the fall in. By now our field guns on the left were barking like so many packs of angry dogs, and as my company was ready first I was again ordered to lead off; it is a bad habit that one, of being ready first.

We marched off, without waiting for the

CH. Ill WE SUPPORT THE FRENCH 17 battalion to close up, along a light railway line for about a mile and a half, and learnt how inconsiderate the British field gunner can be; for firing from about fifty yards on the other side of the railway they appeared to be trying to see how nearly they could miss taking our caps off, doubtless because they resented the fact that we had not already doffed to the inunortal British giumer. And here were some of them actually cooking meat as we were advancing to the storming of Badajoz, or was it Waterloo itself?â nasty fellows, how I hate the smell of cooked meat! and my breakfast had been a biscuit and an inch of chocolate.

Things sounded brisk, and we reached a certain spot where his unemotional highness told our colonel he wished us to dig in. My colonelâ Lord Hampdenâ without any discussion tells me to take my coixipany on half a mile and cover the digging operations of the battalion, and I drew myself up awaiting his valedictory message, and fully expecting him to say, "Good luck! I know 1 can rely on you to hold out to the last whilst the battalion digs in; have you any messages for home? " But this was the only time my colonel disappointed me, and no great and inspiring words did he utter.

C Company therefore pursued its way; and as we approached the brow of a hill I found a good hedgerow, which would at any rate form cover from view, and C Company began to dig in and die.

Now the view looking through this said hedge was interesting; there was a lot doing in the way of shell fire in front, and shells were whistling over our heads from the wrong direction, whilst small parties of Frenchmen could be seen trickling back, which confirmed me in my view tliat we were going to have some shooting. I told the men to dig like beavers, and this they did, in spite of the fact that they had only entrenching tools. I was well armed with a magnificent sword, and I suddenly realised that if these jolly shrapnel chaps began spraying my hedge there was no cover for me, whilst all my lads were already down some inches. So I began to dig in with my sword, and rememberedâ oh ghastly memory 1â that hedge-lines should be avoided, as they are a good target for artillery. Still, if we went in front we should be spotted, and if we dug in in rear we should see nothing, so I stuck to my hedge-line and continued to excavate in this odd manner.

After an hour or so fresh batteries of

French artillery galloped up in rear and began to open fire, and I saw a group of the greatest ruffians life had yet presented to me coming through our lines. They were pale, hairy-faced men in kilts; and as they came to me I realised they were British Highlanders. And then I heard their story. They had been in a bayonet charge in a wood two days before, and had lost their unitâ this was the first sight I had of the defenders of Ypres, and they were not good to look upon; only later did I realise that looks are nothing, and that those unshaven, weary men, were part of the most perfect troops that ever took to fightingâ the British Expeditionary Force.

By the afternoon my lads had dug down well and we began to feel the comfort of earth walls, and at three o clock we heard that only a small section of the French line had given and that a counter attack had regained it. So all was well, and later we would march back to our home of the previous nightâ no Waterloo to-da)

Now I discovered a little farmhouse close by, and in it a dead goat, a sack, and a small pile of bean straw. I left the goat, as he was rather an aged corpse, but I gathered up a nice bundle of bean straw and the suck; and when we marched back I may have looked odd, but that night I lay on bean straw and both my legs went into the sack with bean straw round my feet. After this invention I never parted Avith my sack, and later, in those trying frosty nights, every man in my company had two sand-bags in which he put his feet at night.

During the afternoon we were introduced to Herr Jack Johnson, but we took a dislike to him at first sight. He comes over with a respectable easy-going sound; there is a pause, and then suddenly, with fateful wump, up tears a great volume of smoke with earth and anything else upon which the gentleman alights; and if you go and look where he pitched you find an excavation of circular discription large enough to bury a motor-bus in.

Now Jack Johnson is a sociable fellow, and so he came over with three pals searching for human food. At first I thought it was a sort of ducks-and-drakcs game, as four great explosions followed down a road; but I then learnt that it was a battery of four searching. He is not a tidy chap at all, and throws his excavation sometimes about a quarter of a mile, so that when you are really enjoying him at a distance you may suddenly be felled by a elod of earth or, worse still, a piece of metal, when really you are not part of the show. This is unfair, but I believe not really intended. I am told the best place to be when a Jack Johnson is around is about twenty yards from the edge of his future crater, as then, unless you are concussed, you are not hurt, the effect of his disturbance being chiefly upwards and outwards after his original excavation is completed. But as a rule, people do not attempt to prove this theory.

I often wondered why we heard so much of " coal boxes " in the beginning of the war, but I soon discovered that there was a certain shell not often used, which as it took its airy flight made a noise just as if you were throwing coal out of a scuttle on to the fire. I do not know whether this meant a defective shell or whether it was abandoned by the Huns, but I never heard it after I left Ypres.

Well, by now we had seen lots of things, and personally I had decided that with luck they might be dodged for a fortnight.

During these days the great effort of the Germans to pierce the British line at Ypres was reaching its end, but no one knew when fresh hordes of the Hun would not hurl themselves against our line, and now we were visited by our Divisional General, Sir Charles Munro, who came to our farmhouse.

The general is a typical Great-Briton, with bright eyes, a rugged countenance, middle heiglit, with big shoulders and a cheery way wliich endears him to all he meets. "Well," he said, "I'm glad to see you; how glad perhaps you can reahse when I tell you yesterday my reserves for the division were one platoon!"

Just what this means I doubt if England will ever realise, but I will try inadequately to explain. The 2nd Division, named by our friends the enemy the " Iron Division," after playing a marvellous part in the great retreat, at Landrecies and again on the Aisne, exhausted in all but spirit and wasted to a fraction of its former self in numbers, was then hurried in the great strategic rearrangement to hold the line at Ypres. Here, shelled as no troops had ever been, day after day for weeks, the division bore the brunt of the tremendous efforts of the flower of the Kaiser's army to pierce our line. No story will ever rival that of this unequal contest when, pounded all day and night by an overwhelming mass of metal of hideous sounding high explosives to which we had no reply, these mighty soldiers of Englandâ one man to five yards â stood steady always, and rolled back day after day the massed attacks of an unceasing stream of magnificently trained opponents.

Sometimes here or there a few yards of trench might give, because all the defenders were slain; and then on their way up to their parts of the line a company or two would be gathered together and clear the penetrators out with the bayonet, but never, never once did the line bend before the human avalanche.

These were the days when the enemy advanced singing " Rhineland!" when dense columns would march direct against our line and, as the leading fours rolled over, others marching straight over the bodies of their fellows pressed on, themselves to be withered by the most accurate and highly disciplined fire that a scanty line of defenders had ever exercised.

One day, so I was told, as the Prussian Guards advanced in their columns against our line, the leading fours were seen to be locked arm in arm, and some of the leaders, so rumour had it, marched blindfold, so that they might not fear to press on. But heroic as their attacks were, the Prussian Guards had met their match, for the British Guardsâ Cavan's 4th Guards Brigadeâ were there in front of them, and met them with a deadly fire, like some great dam against which a flood is checked, and they faded away like mist before a gale.

The true odds of the great defence of Ypres will probably never be told, but probably from start to finish some half a million of the absolute pick of the Germans made the most terrific:)unch in history, chiefly against three British divisions of a strength of about 30,000 men. When-British peopleâ you sometimes w onder whether all is well with the nation, turn your thoughts to this grand epic, and your backs will straighten, your chins will elevate a little, and perhaps you will have to bottle a tear of pride when you remember these glorious figures, the saviours of Calais, who rest there, covered lightly by the soil of Ypres.

This, then, was the division in which we found ourselvesâ the 2nd Divisionâ although we had not yet gained contact with our Brigade, the 4th Guards, which was not surprising, because in these fierce days the Guards had themselves been separated in the juggling of the line as each fresh phase of the attack took place; and as for the Brigadier, Lord Cavan, I believe I am right in saying that he was shelled out of four different head-quarters in two days, and so he had no time to pay courtesy visits.

Boche now made a big effort against the Zonnebeke position, and a short part of the line was driven in.

It was on this famous occasion, I believe, that a certain colonel of gunners, finding ihat the Prussian Guard had penetrated a small section of the front, lined up his orderly-room staff, servants, cooks, and any one he could collect in the road, and opened fire on the enemy, thus making

Boche believe that he had run up against a second line. Anyhow, time was given for a counter attack to be collected, and the 52nd (Oxford and Bucks), who had only just been taken out of the line, were recalled. The Irish Guards attacking on the right through a wood with the bayonet, a company of the H. L. I, hurriedly rushed up and the 52nd on the left, the gap was filled and the position restored. When I mention that in this counter attack a field company of R. E. joined in the counter attack to save the situation, the position will be appreciated.

It was to this interesting scene, then, that we were on November 14th ordered to go and relieve the much tired 52nd, and some of our officers were sent on to reconnoitre the position.

We arrived at brigade head-quarters, my impressions of which were a little cottage with several holes in the wall, considerable noise from artillery all round, liquid freezing mud everywhere; and in this scene of noisy desolation two privates of tlie King's (Liverpool Regiment) splasliing tln'ough the mire after an old hen which the guard of our brigade head-quarters apparently considered a disreputable old lady, wliom it was their duty to arrest. Whilst our CO. was powwowing with the colonel of the 52nd we had to wait about in the bitter cold, but on being welcomed into the guard room by the sergeant of the guard we were presented with cups of steaming chicken broth, and I found my sympathies, which had previously been with the hen, wxre now wholly on the side of the guard.

We walked through a wood to see the left of our line, where we joined the King's, and walked down a ride on which our left rested, wliere we paused, and I curiously looked round tlie corner of the wood, when I was yelled at by our colonel friend, who explained that, if I showed myself there, not only would I die from an enemy bullet, but, far more important, the whole party might get slielled! And so it is that we get less curious as we get older. He also explained that half the battalion would rest in this wood whilst the other half was in the trenches, that frequently the wood was shelled and that it was therefore advisable to keep the men in the holes provided for them (dugouts were a later invention, and no one had up to now had time to dig to any depth).

At dusk the battalion arrived, and as soon as it was dark I proceeded with my company overground to my allotted trench, where I relieved a company of the 52nd. Whilst this relief was going on, bullets were spitting and cracking round us all the time, and I thought that many would be hit; but I was green, and as a matter of fact we suffered no casualties.

The so-called trench was for the most part a series of holes, and not at all a nice place for officers, as instead of walking along a trench to see if the sentries were awake, I had to walk continually along the top. To-morrow night 1 vowed that we would scrape some sort of a trench in spite of the zipping of the bullets. The men of the 52nd were amazed at the impudence of a Territorial battalion coming up to hold their lineâ the line of the bloody fight of two days previous, but they were mighty glad to see us for all that, and Territorials went up a point or two in their estimation. That niglit I could not sleep; excitement kept me awake, for the sudden bursts of rifle fire to our riglu and left sliowed tliat liveliness was still in these parts; but I dozed off for a few minutes as I stood in my hole, and then I felt soinething soft and wet pressed against my face. I woke with a start, to hear a strange yet not unfamiliar noise, to discover that an old sow and her litter of pigs had come to pay her call on the Hertfordshire Regiment. I believe that some pork was enjoyed the next evening, but as the nearest inhabitants were miles away, I think that the loot was, under the circumstances, not very wicked.

After this experience I decided to venture into a farmhouse immediately in rear, and told a sentry to come to me half an hour before dawn.

1 struggled through a very muddy yard and was glad to get under a roof, and laying myself down slept in great comfort for two hours. The sentry woke me up, as I thought, rather violently and with a very scared look on his face, and only then,

by the light of a match, did I discover that within a yard of me lay the coipse of a Prussian Guardsman. I stole back to my company, feeling that exploration was not always pleasant, and nearly tripped over several bodies in the yard, where Connaught Rangers and Prussians had been killing each other four days before.

I was glad to get back to my hole, sow or no sow, and there gave the order to stand to. As dawn cameâ our first in the trendiesâ an extraordinary sight unfolded itself, for over the field in front of us were scores of great grey bodies, of the men of the Kaiser's Guard, some lying facing us who had fallen in the attack, others facing away who had been killed when our counter attack took place. Up to now we had most of us felt a good deal of the sport of war, but here we were up against the reality, for all around was death, and we graduated into the ranks of campaigners.

My company was only kept forty-eight hours in these trenches, when we went to the aforementioned wood and were relieved by another company of our battalion. Arriving in the wood late at night we were shown the dugouts in which we were to rest ourselves, but unfortunately we discovered that these residences were not very spacious. Iy first decision, therefore, was to lie outside under the trees; but as bullets began cracking against the trees all round us, I soon came to the conclusion that crushed sleeping quarters were better than the simple life above ground.

The effect of bullets penetrating a wood is very strange until you get accustomed to them, and I remember this night I was under the impression for quite a consider- able time that there were German snipers actually in the wood, firing at us with rifles which made less noise than usual. This was because the crack of the bullet sounded like the crack of a rifle, especially when they hit a tree in one's immediate neighbourhood. Thus at one moment I was almost convinced that a German was firing at me from about thirty yards' distance, and accordingly kept my revolver out and my head down. This is one of the illusions which add to the excitement of the moment, but which is soon exposed. However, that night I slept in a hole with both of my subalterns sleeping on top of me, a most uncomfortable proceeding, but I reasoned it out that my fifteen stone odd, had the position been reversed, would have resulted in no subalterns for C Company the next morning.

The next day, as we were all profoundly convinced that there were snipers in the wood, the two companies quartered there decided to have a drive and to try and bag a German, so they extended through the wood and, in the best covert shooting discipline, drove the wood, but no live Germans were discovered, although we had the satisfaction of learning afterwards that our drive had succeeded to the extent of one German, who fled straight into the Hnes of the King's Liverpool and was duly annexed. The only live German whom we bagged through this tour was an officer of the Prussian Guard, who was found wounded in a hole. He had remained alive since the Prussian Guard attack, and was extremelv s rateful for the care we bestowed upon him and afterwards, I believe, recovered.

We now heard, with great joy, that tlie French were coming up to relieve us; and if we were gladdened by such tidings, just imagine what the feelings must have been of the remainder of the division, who had been in the line nearly a month without relief, and who had had such hard fighting previously.

It was my good fortune to see a good deal of the British regular battalions who were holding the line at this time, and from every point of view the odds against them were such that one wondered how on earth the positions had been held for so long. There was only one thing which surprised one more, and that was the spirit of tlie troops who had seen such a very large proportion of their comrades wiped out, and into whose heads the idea never seems to have entered that the line could possibly be broken by the enemy. This, notwithstanding the fact that the Germans were ten to one, that their artillery outnumbered us at every point, and their heavy guns were pounding our positions continually without any reply of the same description from us!

The regular army knew that it would be months before the new army could be formed, and yet this indomitable little host were so sure of themselves that I firmly believe that none of them would have been surprised if they had been ordered to make a general attack upon the enemyâ " some spirit," as the Americans would say.

The news that the French were coming to relieve the British troops at Ypres spread very quickly through all ranks, and in spite of the bitter cold and wet, every one became very cheerful. Such a big relief could not of course take place all at once, and it was decided to relieve the left of the line where we were first, and I was sent off with two other officers on the morning of the 16th to reconnoitre the route where the French were coming, so as to be able to guide them up to our trenches during the night. We set off across country, and had not gone more than a quarter of a mile before we suddenly found shrapnel falling round us, whereupon we precipitated ourselves upon the earth for a second, jumped up again, when another shrapnel burst right amongst us, one bullet of which penetrated through all the clothes of one of our company

Comm anders without hurting him. We came to the conclusion that the German artillery must be able to see us and were sniping at us with field guns, and accordingly we moved on at a most undignified pace over that piece of country. As a matter of fact, the shelling was chance searching by the Germans and we could not really be seen, but we were still novices at the game. We were directed to go to certain headquarters a mile from our wood, w here we would be told where and when to expect the French. The said head-quarters were a tiny cottage occupied by the head-quarters staff of two historic British battalions. As we entered the little door the scene presented to us will not easily be forgotten.

Under the dim light of one candle some eight officei-s were gathered round a table, and it is hard to imagine signs of greater physical fatigue than were evidenced on their faces; but they were all typical officers of the old regular army: that type which never shows surprise and which considers every question with dignity and without emotion.

I have no hesitation in saying that the greatest strength of the British officer lies in the fact that he is trained, from his earliest 86 RELIEVED BY THE FRENCH pt. i days in the profession, not to get excited and to take things quietly, and I beheve tliat this is one of the principal reasons why regular officers have such a great ascendancy over their men, for the appearance of silent strength under any circumstances must give confidence in war.

Walking into this cottage in our comparatively smart khaki with polished buttons, and finding ourselves amongst these men witli the distant look in their eyes which comes from continual strain, we felt we had entered a new world. No one announced they were glad to see us or asked us any curious questions; no one patronised us as Territorials; we were simply treated as if we were members of the mess who came in every day to report for orders. Our friends soon served us with steaming cups of cocoa, whilst we sat in that little room crushed up into a small spaceâ how often in future were we to be crushed into small spaces! As we sat we discussed the question of the relief by the French, and we were stroncrlv reconmiended to recon-noitre a cross-country route in order to save the French two miles of road that was almost impossible owing to the mud, and having been directed, off we went to the point where we were to meet the French later in the day, and thence we reconnoitred the route we had to go.

Sights in that wood will not easily be forgotten, for it was here where the Germans temporarily gained a footing in our line and had been driven out by a bayonet attack. By marking trees we came to the conclusion that we would be reasonably certain to find our way in the night. In order to make this short cut, however, part of the route was just behind some trenches held by the Northamptonshire Regiment. We were somewhat dismayed to see that we should have to take the whole battalion of Frenchmen across a field where they would not be 300 yards from the enemy, so we made up our minds that somehow we must convey this fact to our French friends when we took them up.

There was a stable and cottage by the side of the road where we had to wait for the French, but the stable was by no means sweet, so we lay down in the road; but as it became dark we discovered that the road was a most unhealthy place, since bullets came ripping our way continually, and occasionally a Maxim gun swept straight along it, so we tucked ourselves under a wall 38 RELIEVED BY THE FRENCH pt. i in as sheltered a place as we could be whilst the bullets spluttered against the cottage. Whilst we were waiting here we saw stretcher parties going by with various British woundedâ that procession which had gone by daily for nearly a month and which, after to-night, would be no longer a British procession.

At last a messenger came to tell us that the French were approaching, and we went out to meet them. The battalion lay down on the side of the road whilst the French commandant, with his officers, came into the stable to make his dispositions for the relief. A candle was produced, and there Mons. le Commandant and his officers, none of whom knew a word of English, wrestled with us, who knew hardly a word of French, over the intricacies of the relief operation which was about to take place. After about three-quarters of an hour, by the use of maps and pigeon language, the whole thing was cleared up, and we struck up a great friendship with our French comrades, who shook us repeatedly by the hand, but for some reason or other did not offer to kiss us. After finally imploring them with many gesticulations to impose silence upon their men and to non fumer, which we imagined was an injunction not to smoke, we set off on our night's march.

The Frenchmen behaved very well in going by the difficult spot, and they might have been a thousand n)ice. But when we got into the wood the whole battalion got very animated, and I comforted myself by reflecting that such was the noise that the enemy would be under the impression that a large number of jays had returned to those parts. Whenever we passed what was once a German soldier, the Frenchmen, in single file, could be heard uttering what, I am sure, were terrible oaths, right back to the end of the battalion; equally if we passed a dead Englishman, they would give expression to their feelings of compassion.

Having eventually reached the edge of the wood, we were about 100 yards from the right of my battalion; but as we were coming from the right front, where the line bent forward and there was a small gap, I was rather anxious that the Herts Regiment should not test its marksmanship upon us, so I crawled forward to where I knew there was an isolated post, suddenly to hear a very fierce whisper and to observe 40 RELIEVED BY THE FRENCH pt. i a bayonet flashing under the moon, challenging me. However, having assured the sentry that we were decent folk, up to no mischief, I went back and brought the French along. The relief was carried out without any difficulty, each Frenchman tumbling into his hole as our men climbed out. The French commandant, instead of sleeping in a dugout, insisted that he would go and sleep in my farmhouse of three nights before. I used all my persuasiveness, and invented wonderful words to explain to him the horrors of that non-bon place; but apparently the French officer, even if a house is known to be shelled at all times or possesses other residential drawbacks, prefers to sleep therein to anywhere else.

By this time it was late at night, and our battalion began to march back to the rest trenches which we had previously occupied at Kilometre 3 on tiie Ypres-Menin Road. The road was in an indescribable state, slimy chalk mud about half a foot deep, and there were a nasty number of bullets flying about.

When we reached Weston Hoek we were delayed for a long time, as various British regiments marched back on relief. The road was very congested and movement slow, and as Boche began shelling we were not very delighted at our enforced wait whilst the endless stream passed us on the main road. Meanwhile, we heard that our medical cart had got bogged and was temporarily abandoned. We did, however, at last arrive back at Kilometre 3, and there, to my joy, I heard that my company was to have the privilege of going to the farm, and it was not long before C Company was fast asleep, and noticeably its commander, who had been on the go for over eleven consecutive hours after four nights of little sleep.

Blessed are those who are not luxurious, for they shall have a peaceful time!

As I explained, my company now had the luxury of the farm building, and we had the laugh of the rest of the battalion, which lay down to rest in the freezing mud. We had a comfortable night, my bed being that on which many a weary cow had laid herself to rest. We rose late for our ablutions, feeling very peaceful in mind, when suddenly we heard a whistling through the air, followed by a most terrific explosion which was evidently somewhere inside the farm. The whole of the company was immediately got out of the building and ordered to double to the trenches; but before they had all got clear from the farm, another shell of similar gigantic proportions exploded, killing one lad and knocking over half a dozen others. I was still in the cows' stall, hastily donning my puttees, when a third shell pitched into the yard itself, and the air was a mass of debris all around. I called out to the three officers' servants who were left in the stables to get clear of the building at once and ran to the door, where I discovered a terrified horse belonging to one of our mounted officers, tied up to the wall; and it was fortunate for me that it was so, as I jumped on his back and galloped, and had only just cleared the farmyard when a fourth shell pitched right on the stable which I had just left. All three of the officers' servants had been badly wounded, and we decided to keep away from these farm buildings in future.

There is no doubt that some German aeroplane had spotted this farm and had directed their 8-inch guns to fire upon it, and the shooting was indeed remarkable. The farmhouse itself was not touched, and the old Belgian farmer and his wife, with three young refugees, continued to live in this house and to farm their land regardless of the warning which they had received.

We now continued to live a very crowded existence in the rest trenches, whilst all the time the enemy kept throwing heavy stuff all around us.

The same afternoon we had an unexpected order to march to Zillebeke to relieve the 10th Hussars and the Royals, who were holding that part of the line.

We were feeling anything but fresh before we started on our march to Zillebekeâ not that we had taken any exercise, but there is nothing more tiring than to sit still all day in poor shelters under heavy shelling, and especially is this true of new troops, who think that every shell is specially directed at them and who can hardly distinguish the noise of the burst of an enemy shell from that of their own guns. After a time the experienced soldier knows when a shell is high up or going to his flanks, and realises that not every missile that hurtles through the air has his own name and number inscribed thereon.

Soon after dusk we moved off along a slimy road, whilst the night got colder and colder. After dodging many shell holes, which we had difficulty in discerning owing to the liquid mud that filled them, we came to

Zillebeke village, or what remained of it. A battered church still looked like a church, houses dishevelled and war-broken still stood tottering or with roof stripped bare; but ruin, stark ruin, seemed to stare at us from every side. In many of these residences, where cover remained, little groups of Frenchmen could be seen warming thumbs round bright fires, and very picturesque they looked in their baggy red trousers. It was a mystery whence these Frenchmen came or to what units they belonged, but they seemed at any rate to be masters of the art of making themselves at home, and there were many little tricks we decided to pick up from poilu before the weeks got much older.

The traffic on the road was thick, and it was some time after dark when we arrived at Zillebeke Wood, where guides met us and we continued our serpentine march to the trenches.

The moon was now out and a hard frost had set in as we wended our way through the pine trees until we came to a comfortable looking dugout, and the battalion was halted whilst company commanders were ordered up.

Very cosy within looked the dugout as we entered to get our orders and were introduced to the squadron commanders of the 10th and the Royals whom we were to reheve.

We were soon moving on again on the side of a little valley, down which rushed a little stream, and our guides passed the word ' No smoking or talking! " We came to a ride which was swept at times, so we were told, by a machine gunâ my pace was smarter across that rideâ and so on until we got to the line. Here again no trench, just holes to hold two or three men, and very quickly we slid in as the cavalrymen climbed out. My Hussar guide told me that we must be careful in the davtime, as we were only sixty yards from the Hun. " Really," I replied, in a voice which pretended to be barely interested as I stood there three-score yards from Bocheland, whilst bullets spat every few seconds through the trees.

"Yes," said the phlegmatic one, " they attacked this morning, but they can't rush you; there are so many trees down you can hear them tumble; besides, we have hung a lot of jam tins on the wire."

"Will you go away, man, and let me get into my hole?" I whispered fiercely to myself when at last he said, "Well, I must be getting on. Poor had your dugout; he was killed this morning, shot through the brain. It is absurd saying the Bodies cannot shoot."

"Quite absurd," I answered. " Goodnight!"

The night became more frosty and we could clearly hear Boche talking over there, when suddenly, away on our right, rifles began to crack, and then in the quiet of that wood the cracking was taken up far to the right and rolling right along in a crescendo of sound till our men joined in; and again, then on our left, and the roar of thousands of rifles echoed through the night whilst the split-splut thud of German ball anmiuni-tion played over our heads. We of course imagined that the enemy were attacking. After a while the firing died down again, but twice during that night heavy firing started, and again the crescendo of din occurred, but this time it was the Huns; and as we knew we were not attacking, we merely stood to with our heads well down and assured each other that the enemy had " got the wind up."

In the early hours of the morning rations were brought along and had to be dis-tributed in the open, whilst a lot of rifle firing went on, and one began to realise how much lead can hurtle without finding its mark.

All ranks stood to early, and we awaited dawn in a hard frost and discovered the bolts of our rifles in many cases jammed by the freezing of the mud with which they had got covered in the night.

Just as the light of day was coming, and whilst we still could hardly discern any object clearly and trees looked like men, I heard a faint rustle in front of me; then suddenly, not thirty yards to my front, I saw a hel-metted German, looking huge in the half light, stand straight up to step over a fallen tree; my hand was on my rifle, and I aimed; crack! and down he fell, just as sentries right and left of me also let drive, and the Hertfordshires accounted for their first Hun.

As I explained there was no trench, and all orders had to be passed along the line. I am sure this brave German had heard me passing orders, and had come to bag me in the half light, just as he had probably killed my predecessor in my hole the preceding day.

As daylight came, we began to see where we were, and very beautiful the wood looked with its coating of frost. Our position ran to my left fairly straight, but 100 yards to my right it bent back at right angles across a ride, where we had a good view through the wood for about 600 yards; and here, during the day, our right company got some good long-distance shooting, as numerous Germans could be seen doubling across the ride, especially in the evening, when our lads claimed several hits, and we got a machine gun into action down the ride after dark.

Early the next morning German aeroplanes were playing about in the sun over our heads, and we wondered why they should hover over us in this attentive manner.

We were not long left in doubt. For several hours our right company was subjected to a shelling by German heavies, such as would have tested any troops in the world.

The shooting was remarkably accurate, and soon casualties were reported in rapid succession as Jack Johnsons fell all round the holes in which our lads were trying to take cover. Great masses of earth were hurled into the air to crash down all along the line; trees fell, and we, who were only 100 yards away, could only watch in silence what looked like the decimation of our comrades.

At midday I had a message thrown along from hole to liole in an empty jam tin to tell me that the company commander and his subaltern were both buried, and asking for orders.

Now they were at the apex of a triangle, and I thought that this shelling was probably the prelude to an attack, so I sent the first order which had ever made me hate myself, to the effect that they were to hang on, and that I would endeavour to replace their casualties. I sent back to another company commander to send up fifty men to reinforce our battered right; and whilst the inferno continued, the reinforcements came steadily up through the trees and lay down in the open wood just behind the trouble. Gradually they rushed, one at a time, through the danger zone, and so the gaps were filled. The attack which we had expected all day never came, and so our comrades went unavenged.

Of this company which had been so badly hammered, seven were killed by shell fire, two were never seen again and believed to be buried, seven were dug out alive, and some twelve others wounded.

We were much impressed with the necessity of a communication trench, which up to then, owing to the scarcity of men, had not been dug, since owing to our proximity to the enemy we were cut off from headquarters, and stretcher bearers and orderhes had little chance of getting through alive.

At seven o'clock that night the 2nd Coldstream Guards relieved us, and right glad we were, after a long and weary wait, to stagger back, shaken, cold, and thirsty, to our rest trenches on the Ypres-Mcnin Road.

Rest, real rest, away from this clamour and dinâ how good that message was, for since we had been hurled into the vortex of this strange world, we had never been for a moment out of shell fire. We had seen men die, we had fed solely on bully beef and biscuits, and we had been either soaked to the skin or blue with coldâ (I almost said funk).

All day long the French came trickling along the cobbled road from Ypres, fine fellows, laden with their heavy equipment, but not too heavy to prevent their carrying kettles and pots to add to their " Father Christmas " appearance.

The French tread very liglitly, and they never march in step except through a town or on parade; and often riding along in the dark I have found myself on top of a stealthy French battalion marching in such different style to the steady tramp of our British troops; but they cover the ground well, and the regular regiments of the French Army give one a great feeling of confidence as they move quietly about their work without any fuss.

We had a good sample of French coolness as we watched them tliis dav, for whilst they marched along the road a battery of Jack Johnsons suddenly opened with salvos along the road, and the French battalion very soon scattered into artillery formation of little groups of eight men in the fields on either side of the road. There was no confusion and no apparent alarm when suddenly a shell burst right in front of a little group; three men fell dead, one retired back wounded, and the other four calmly put the dead in the crater made by the shell, covered them up, placing a loose piece of wood to mark the spot, and then walked quietly on.

We had to wait till niglit for orders to march, and I returned with two brother officers to the farm from whicli I had fled so precipitately a few days before, to see if I could get a hot drink. The old Belgian farmer and liis plucky wife were still there, clinging with the persistence of madness to all they had lived for; and there, in one of the only rooms left standing, the little wrinkled old woman gave us huge bowls of steaming coffee.

Just as we were fully engrossed in this joyful task, suddenly crash, crash, crash, tiles flew and the house shook, but all the old lady said was " Bon, bon, shrapnel shrapnel," as she poured out more coffee. So this wonderful old lady could express pleasure that only shrapnel was crashing on her home and not high explosives which would finally destroy her! War indeed teaches us to see the proportion of things.

Their stable was flattened, half their house a mass of ruins, their barn now possessed one wall, and yet, indomitable so il, she could utter " Bon, bon, shrapnel! " I myself saw two men killed and five wounded in their very yard, but what happened to these two wonders I never heard; all I do know is that for those three bowls of coffee three golden sovereigns were gladly offered, and three British officers were sad to leave such brave hearts who had been caught in the clutches of war, but refused to flee the home of their ancestors.

We waited wearily for those orders which never came, until at last at 10.45 p. m. the message reached us. An orderly had tried to find VIS earlier, but whichever way he went he met a barrage of shell fire and had to go some miles round.

Off at last, where we did not know, but we knew it was for rest, and that is a wondrous place.

To reach the main road we had to go in the pitch dark by a side track, and here a big shell had made an enormous excavation right across the road, leaving only a goat path for the infantry to creep by; but it was my job to see the battalion past. Fortunately the transport had gone on early, but there were still the pack-horses and the medical cart to negotiate this obstacle. By informing the pack-horses that they were goats, we managed to get them all by except one " unbeliever" which slithered down to the bottom of the crater, and all the King's horses and all the King's men could not extract that pack-horse. The medical cart was clearly checkmated, and so I left the doctor to wait for dawn and bring the pack-horse if he could; this with the help of ropes he achieved early next morning.

What a march! By this time the head of the battalion must have nearly reached Ypres, and I was unable at first to catch the last company to ask leave to close up. The road was a sheet of ice and the pack-horses went down one after the other; it was pitch dark; two French battalions were passing us and a British cavalry regiment marching across the road, but at last I caught the rear of the column and passed up the word to halt.

Once m-ore we marched through Ypres, but how changed from our last visit! This time whole rows of houses were in ruins, and the Cloth Hall was shatteredâ its ancient beauty gone for ever. The night was very cold, the wind cutting like a knife, and as we marched on down country roads men began to fall out, only to be cursed on again by my brutal self, for I knew that we had fifteen miles to go, and that a man who dropped now out, far away from houses and with no British troops behind, would suffer privation and worse, because to lie there that bitter night and sleep meant death.

At last, with few men out, we saw ahead great bonfires at Ouderdom, the half-way halt where we knew hot drinks awaited us.

Here the congestion was great, and it was another hour before we got to our field. Tommy, you are a strange fellow! No sooner did he lay down his kit, weary, cold, with frost-bitten feet, than he starts to sing, and all the world's a schoolyard and all the men are boys.

Tea is served out and a tot of rum, and for an hour we sing and try to get warm round the great fires and talk of rest. Now we are off again for Meteren in falling snow; the narrow roads are choked with traffic and we have to move in single file for miles. The men are " sticking it " well, but half the battalion is limping, and just as dawn breaks we begin to scale Mont Noir. Here on the steep ascent some scores of men drop out, for frostbite had found its victims. My horse does a side slip on the icy surface â crash we both go, but no bones broken and on again; now we are on the sunmiit of the liill and the sun is up. The view is beautiful, for miles around appears a glorious landscape of snow-clad plains of Flanders, but the faces of our men are not beautiful; haggard and pale they struggle on, with pain in their every step.

Many men of many regiments are on the side of the road. They all have the war look!

that look which I, a stranger, had seen when we came to Ypres, a look which I had never seen before or since, and which I hope never to see again.

So we came south from the first defence of Ypres.

Our stay at Meteren gave us a good chance of reorganisation, and we quickly pulled ourselves together. At first we found that quite 50 per cent, of the men were unable to march owing to frostbite; but luckily the trouble was only incipient, and after a week the whole battalion was on its feet again.

We now had opportunities of making the acquaintance of our brigadeâ the 4th (Guards)â and very welcome we were made, all ranks going out of their way to show that our intrusion was not resented. At first we were inclined to be astonished to see the Guards practising the slow march and other ceremonial movements in muddy fields, as I think we imagined we had left all that kind of thing behind; but it was not long before we followed suit and learnt the lesson which we never forgot, that steady drill after the trenches is the one way to keep discipline and " snap."

We received the following message from Brigadier-General the Earl of Cavan, commanding the 4th Guards Brigade:

The Brigadier would like to take this opportunity of welcoming the 1st Battalion Hertfordshire Regiment to the Brigade. From what he has already seen in the trenches and on the march, he is certain that the battalion will play a noble part in this great war. The battalion has already had hard work and lost some good comrades, but they left with their line intact, which is an achievement fit to rank in history with other great battles of the Army.

On November 23rd the brigade was inspected by the Commander-in-Chief, who addressed in turn the 2nd Grenadiers, 2nd Coldstream, 3rd Coldstream, 1st Irish, and Herts.

On this occasion we were almost ashamed of our strength, as we were far the strongest unit on parade, one of the Guards battalions parading only some eighty strong, commanded by a captain who brought them out of Ypres. Sir John French spoke with no little emotion when he thanked these gallant remnants of the pick of our manhood for the wonderful part they had played; but it was sad to remember how many of these magnificent "six-footers" had gone West, and that they had done their part to save the line at such a terrible cost.

At the end of November the troops were inspected by His Majesty the King, and although the weather was cold and Flanders looked its bleakest, it was an inspiring sight to see the long straight roads lined on either side by endless walls of khaki, topped by the glint of thousands of bayonets.

The King, with the Prince of Wales, General Officers, and Staff, walked down the whole line, and each company hailed him with tumultuous cheers as he reached its head. I do not know whether one may attribute thoughts to a King, but I believe he was proud that day, as his soldiers were proud of him. A few gracious words to commanding officers, and he passed on to fresh cheering ranks of other brigades. " God save the King!"

This life of ease had to come to an end soon, and on December 22nd we were ordered to march to Bcthunc, where troublous times were occurring.

In the early hours of the morning the 4th Brigade assembled for the long march of nineteen miles to Bethune, near which town a very heavy attack had been made upon the Indian troops. To the Hertfordshires was given the honour of heading the brigade, and this put the battalion on their mettle, with the result that they reached their destination with only some ten men left on the road. For a considerable part of the way the Prince of Wales marched at the head of the Hertfordshire Regiment with our colonel. When we arrived at the outskirts of Bethune it was already dark, and we lay down on the banks of the canal waiting for orders as to billeting. It was a very quiet night, and a well-known songster in our battalion stood up by the side of the canal and began to sing with great success, the chorus being taken up by the 64 FOR FIGHTING PASTURES NEW pt. i whole brigade, and the effect was most striking. The British soldier is fond of singing in the dark, but by day only a few bold spirits take to song. At last our billeting parties sent guides, and the march proceeded to Bethune. The battalion marched through the town as if they had come two miles instead of nineteen, and the whole of the inhabitants, hearing our marching songs, turned out to welcome the brigade, and it was quite exciting to all of us once more to see the bright shop windows and evidences of civilisation. We proceeded to the tobacco factory, where we found a large number of Indian troops already ensconced, and many of them were seen in the yard, squatting round little fires where they cooked marvellous Eastern dishes, greatly to the interest of all ranks of ours, many of whom had never before seen an Indian soldier.

Very early the next morning the brigade marched to Les Facons, where we had our dinners during a slight snow storm in a muddy field, and at dusk we moved up close into support of the line, where we went into some farm buildings, and on December 24th, officers were ordered forward to reconnoitre the line.

The trenches we were about to take over were held by a battahon of Jats, and we were shown round the Hne by one of the four white officers left in this unit. The trenches were poor and wide, the Indians having had to dig in in a hurry along old ditches, which are always places to be avoided if time permits to entrench elsewhere. The Jat is a tall, handsome looking fellow, and has made quite a reputation on this front as a steady soldier, but it was pitiful to see how much they evidently felt the damp coldâ indeed, it was a good thing they were to be relieved, because, as their officers told us, they had had a bad gruelling, and it is not good to hold a line when many of your comrades lie dead out in front.

In this particular sector there was a sap running out 150 yards in front of the line to within ten yards of a German sap, and here daily a British officer of this corps went up to snap shoot at the enemy with his revolver, just by way of showing how much kick the Jats had left in them.

These turbaned gentlemen, with their silky straight black hair, were very happy to think we were coming to see their habitation with a view to occupation, and the trenches became animated with chatter and much amiable advice to keep our heads down.

On the way back to the battalion, the enemy began to shell Dead Cow Farm and Chocolat Menier Corner. The former name needs no explanation; the latter was a crossroad in the Rue du Bois, where the advertisement of the famous firm stared you in the face on the wall of a corner house.

Now these high-explosive shells walked down the road with us, so to speak, as if to convey the intimation, "Nasty place this you have come to!"

A brother officer and I at the third ' crump," which was in the yard of one of the houses about fifty yards off, began to run, but just at that moment a stream of Ghurkas came rushing out of their threatened billets, and so we had to pull up sharp and walk very deliberately, pausing here and there to admire the scenery; however, the next shell was some way off, so that our dignity was not put to the supreme test, and we strolled on whilst Johnnie Ghurka returned to his house.

The line was relieved at night, and our tall friends, with a goodly display of beautiful white teeth, silently faded away as we made ourselves at home in their trenches and wondered whether the North Pole was really cold.

There was a big gap away on our left, but as we had no maps except for our immediate trenches, we did not know that a thousand yards to our left the line bent forward almost at right angles, and that we were on the circumference of a semicircle.

An hour or two after we were settled down that night a fairly heavy rifle fire opened on us from our left, and as I was in charge of the battalion in the line, I ordered rapid fire in order that these dogs of Huns might be silenced. We plumped lead into the void, and they fired back with some spirit, and so for half an hour the fire fight went on until I ordered the cease fire.

Only next morning did I discover that this fiercely contested battle had been joined, not with the detested Germans, but with His Britannic Majesty's most loyal and gallant Highland Light Infantry, and that the total casualties were, Herts Regiment, nil., H. L. I, nil. I had to explain to the officers of our company that I thought they should correct their fire three-quarters right next night, as I feared they did not quite realise where their front was!

Little did I think during the year of 1902, when I was attached for several weeks to the H. L. I. as their guest, that 1914 would find me in a foreign land, ordering rapid fire on their devoted heads; and I really had no grudge, for their hospitality was always lavish; but they " hit me first," as the little boy always explains on these occasions.

Our first Christmas in the trenches was celebrated at dawn with rapid fire, and the festival was lively. Early in the day I got news that a lad who lived in my native town in Hertfordshire had been killed by a bullet whilst on sentry in the sap, and then it was that a sergeant in his company anxiously asked and received leave to go up and take his place.

The sergeant, who was a good shot, avenged the boy by killing the German sniper; but shortly afterwards a bullet through the brain sent him to join his young comrade. After this we began to study the art of sniping, and the tactics of the hunter were added to the science of shooting.

It was a cold, sharp day, and we received various gifts which friends at home had sent to us, and many a charcoal fire was busy cooking wonderful dishes along the trench.

That night both sides sang carols, and the firing ended.

We had a small right-angled salient in our line, and we decided to dig a new and better trench in front to cut off the angle, and so we sallied forth one night into No Man's Land to start this work.

We waited until it was dark, and then the first party scrambled out over the parapet. A listening post crawls out in front to guard against the coming of the Hun and silently we line up where the new trench is to be dug. Just as the first party are " dressed " for digging, up goes a German star shell, and No Man's Land is as bright as Regent Street in nights of peacetime. Down we all flop until the constellation is over, and then to work. Bullets idly ping over our heads as the work proceeds, and soon our first party are down half a foot, and another party steals out and lines up on our right. Confidence soon reigns, and the earth begins to fly. Boche has not spotted us, and so the star shells are not followed by the crackle of machine guns.

After two hours the digging reliefs come out and drop into the holes already dug, whilst the first parties slip back to the trenches.

The moon comes up, but now we are getting down to our work, and a respectable parapet is rising; and so the work goes on till dawn, when we all creep back to the trench.

Very proud we were of our first night's work and not a single casualty to report. After a night or two the trench is practically complete and we man our new line, feeling far safer in the deep, well-traversed trench, and we all are proud of our architectural feat. Have we not advanced the line and shortened it by a hundred yards!! The new Une has to be wired, and this is more dangerous work, for we had to hammer in our wooden stakes, and you have not the consolation which the digger possesses of knowing that every minute you work you get farther under cover.

Night after night, right along the scores of miles of British front, Uttle parties are always working on the wireâ it is the least popular job in the war, but it has to be done, and the good battauon never vacates the line with gaps in the wire.

I mentioned that we had a sap within ten yards of the Germans. In reality it was a ditch with two mud walls, each wall with loopholes, one mud wall held by the Germans and one by ourselves.

This was before the days of bombs, and as one stood in the sap the garrison of the enemy could be clearly heard talking and coughing. I tried sometimes to gain some news from these gentlemen by addressing them in English, to the effect that they had far better surrender now before the vast British Armies arrived on the scene, but all I got for my trouble were guttural oaths, only a few of which I could understand. I had to visit this sap once by day and once by night for fourteen days; it was a fascinating spot, but of this more anon.

After Christmas we had to fight the elements. Our trenches, as I said, were really ditches, and here the waters began to gather. All through the night fatigue parties from the companies in rear brought hurdles and fascines, and all the time, night after night, we fought the waters. One day we would succeed in getting a dry footing all along the trench, but the rains continued and by night our temporary flooring had disappeared in the mud.

The sap was even worse, and the last few days in the line we could not get to the post without getting wet to the middle. This was an amazing midnight bath, but it is wonderful how little sickness occurs on these occasions. Many nights I lay down for an hour or two, Hterally soaked to the skin, and soon dropped off to sleep, and even then sleep was disturbed. This is a typical description of a night in those days.

Retire to " rest " at midnight.

12.45 a. m. Buzâ beâ beâ buzâ buzâ buzâ buz. that beastly telephone againâ perhaps it is not for me. Close eyes again. Please, sir, Captain says

B. Company's rations have not arrived. Ring up Head-quarters and learn that "fatigue party got lost; rations just started for trenches."

1. a. m. Lie down again.

1.45 a. m. Buzâ beâ beâ buzâ buz. Please, sir, telegram from Head-quarters. Message as follows: " Brigade asks have all men received Princess Mary's gifts, and for immediate answer please." I repeat the telegram to all companies and lie down again.

c Â yreplies received from companies.

2.20 a. m.

2.39 a. m.

2.40 a. m. Reply sent to Battalion Headquarters, and I lie down again.

2.57 a. m. Adjutant wants you on the 'phone, sir. He cannot understand your message. I reply to the adjutant and he down again.

5 a. m. Telegram from Division, sir, re- quiring return of gum-boots. Return sent, and lie down again at 5.15.

6 a. m. Time for stand to, sir.

No, dear reader, I did not swear.

O ye great men upon the Brigade Staff, O ye greater men upon the Divisional Staff, O ye wonderful great men upon the Corps Staff, O ye amazing great men upon the Army Staff, O ye greatest of all great men at G. H. Q., have mercy upon the regimental officer in the night season, and grant him, if possible, two, three, or if possible, four hours' sleep, so that he may dream of chateaux and red tabs.

We went out for six days' rest on January 2nd, and it rained almost incessantly, so that we rather shivered at the idea of going back to our next trenches, which were in front of Richebourg, where we experienced the full power of Flanders mud.

We found that what had been trenches were now nothing but rivers, and only a few posts or " islands " were held in front, the actual firing-line troops being quartered in houses in the Rue du Bois.

On either side of the road were substantial brick cottages, which still gave good cover from the weather, and these we proceeded to fortify.

The street itself was an unhealthy spot, as we were directly enfiladed from Port Arthur away on our left, and bullets hummed along the street in some numbers, especially at night.

Here we lost an officer killed whilst visiting the sentries, and a few other casualties. We relieved the posts as frequently as possible, and half the battalion was billeted back in Richebourg, where they were busily engaged in building strong posts.

A company reported on coming out of the advanced posts that they had surprised a working party in the early morning, the fog lifting very rapidly. They were able to pour rapid fire into the Germans, and account, they think, for seven before they got back to their lines.

This company also reported two men missing. In the morning they turned up and told their story, which was that coming back from their island they thought they would use an old communication trench as there was considerable firing, and as a result one of them got bogged, and the other, who went to rescue him, also got bogged, and there they stayed all night unable to get help. In the morning they were dug out by the Irish Guards who had relieved us, and two half-frozen, blue-looking individuals limped back to billets. We wrapped them up in several blankets and sent them to hospital, but I fear they suffered severely.

From Richeboufg we went back to our old line of Christmas-tide and relieved the 60th Rifles under Colonel Northey, who has since won fame in East Africa, and a sad state our old trenches were in. Here again we held the line lightly, and all relief had to be overground after dark, whilst the supports dwelt in some old farms in rear, known to us as Carlton House Terrace.

Piccadilly and Pall Mall, which we thought we had made into fine communication trenches, were now brooks, and the fascinating sap where we conversed with the Germans had been abandoned as hopeless.

The enemy was busy working on his trenches, and during this tour we got some good sniping. I got a shot at a German, but he signalled a " wash out," and disappeared.

Carlton House Terrace was rather lively, and we had three men hit by a machine gun, which was evidently determined to make all suffer who patronised the " West End."

We were reheved by the 2nd Grenadiers, and it was rather an anxious relief, as the ground was white with snow and all reliefs were over the top. The old trenches had to be crossed by bridges which we had put in in the last few nights, and I remember one company of Grenadiers had just crossed a bridge and closed up in a field in rear of the front trench, when a Boche searchlight suddenly switched right on to them. For a moment I thought their dark mass must be discovered and ducked, expecting a hail of bullets, as w e were not more than 150 yards from the enemy, but all was quiet, and the procession continued silently to the front line, where man by man they slid down to pass to their posts, whilst the Herts as silently climbed out and marched back. One incident I remember caused me amusement and indignation whilst in this line. I had told all companies in the morning that working parties should be fired on invariably if detected. That night I was walking round to visit the islands in the front line, and feeling lonelyâ one always feels lonely when one is by oneself at night â when a platoon commander of ours evidently recognised me walking in the snow just in rear of them. To show his ardour he ordered rapid fire on a working party which I fear may have been imaginary; anyhow, the effect was an immediate retort from Hun-land in like coin, and the air was alive with humâ zipâ crackâ swish, whilst I deposited myself in a shell hole which was two feet deep with water. The keen subaltern is sometimes rather a trial!

One had strange meetings on the occasion of these reliefs. As I peered through the darkness to find the officer commanding a company of Grenadiers whom I heard coming along the road, I suddenly found myself face to face with a neighbour in Hertfordshire, Captain Gosselin, with whom I had hunted and shot for many years past, but alas, never again! for, gallant soul, he met his death whilst tending the wounds of a man in his company under a heavy shell fire. My next visitor at Carlton House Terrace, as if he had walked out of the Carlton Club, was Captain Percy Clive, M. P., who to-day is on crutches, but whom all soldiers and M. P."s hope will soon be well.

So do those who remind one of a former existence roll up in the snow-clad mud of Flanders.

Towards the end of January our Colonel, Lord Hampden, left for England to command a brigade, and the responsibility now devolved on my shoulders. There was considerable liveliness in these parts, and we found ourselves on the road several days rising before dawn and marching from Hin-gette, where we were billeted, to points about two miles in rear of Givenchy on the La Bassee Canal, or at Essars, and there we waited all day whilst little rumours came our way about big efforts of the enemy to wrest from our troops Cuinchy and Givenchy, which are on the ridge that stops the road of the Huns to Bethune.

We learnt that the enemy had taken the brickstacks at Cuinchy, and had actually entered the village of Givenchy, to be cleared out again by the vigorous use of Welsh bayonets.

One day I received a message from Brigadier-General the Earl of Cavan, G. O. C. 4th Guards Brigade, ordering commanding officers to attend his head-quarters for a conference. Lord Cavan is one of those exceptional personalities who give confidence from the first moment you meet them, but unlike most famous generals and admirals he makes you feel his friendship at once, and you realise that you are dealing with a very human man. wshort in stature, very strongly built, with a somewhat large head, he meets you with a merry twinkle in his eyes, and you find a rather unusual type of soldier, master of hounds, statesman, leader, and friend all rolled into one.

This was the first serious discussion at which I had met him. Pointing to the map he showed us where the enemy had advanced, and then said quite simply, "We will take back this culvert here, those trenches there, and then those brickstacks up to that point." Then followed instructions to each battalion and orders as to reconnaissance.

The whole description was wonderfully simple, and the orders were given in such a way that not one of us doubted they would prove successful. So it turned out, 82 ATTACK ON THE BRICKSTACKS pt. i for a more perfectly conceived and executed little series of operations could not be imagined.

After reminding the Guards' commanding officers that their men were very bigâ always a matter of pride to this little manâ he dismissed us with a cheery word, and we jumped on our horses and rode back to our units, feeling that almost already the brickstacks were ours.

My impressions at the time were not that I had been listening to a great genius, but that I had been talking to a man who was full of common sense; since then, however, I have come to ask whether, after all, the greatest genius is not the man who possesses the biggest fund of that most valuable quality. How many lives would be saved if common sense always ruled, and the possible and impossible were realised by all leaders.

The brigade now moved up to the Cuinchy area, the 3rd Coldstream and Irish Guards into the line, with the Herts in close support, and the 2nd Grenadiers and 2nd Coldstream in reserve.

During the first few nights we were busily engaged in burying the dead who were lying about from the previous fighting.

and the brigadier was most particular that allâ British and Germansâ should be carried out of the lines and buried in cemeteries in rear. It was dangerous work and trying to young hands, but we carried back across the open over a hundred dead, and gave them decent burial.

The temptation is to bury on the spot, but the disadvantages are so great that an effort is always made, if the enemy's guns permit, to carry the dead on stretchers to selected cemeteries, where great care is taken to mark and preserve the graves of the fallen.

This attack was the first occasion on which concentrated artillery was used in a surprise bombardment, and it must be remembered that, in spite of the eloquent speeches of a certain statesman, in which he assured the country that we had enough ammunition, in reality we had hardly any ammunition at all, and the enemy pounded us all day whilst we were unable to reply.

On this occasion Lord Cavan and our Divisional General, Major General Home, the famous gunner who now commands the 1st Army, had managed to get quite a formidable array of heavies, and for those days a considerable amount of ammunition.

Our guns were all concentrated so as to 84 ATTACK ON THE BRICKSTACKS pt. i bring converging fire to bear on the objective, which was only about half a mile wide, and the heavies opened a deliberate fire during the morning upon the Boche positions.

There were noises new to us, as 9-inch and 15-inch shells moaned their way over our heads, and the dull roar of their explosions followed in quick succession. Now the 60-pounders gave tongue with a sharp crack, and the field howitzers, with unassuming voice, joined in the chorus.

Our battalion lay in wait just under the Cuinchy ridge, and at midday I had orders to move two companies up. They moved across the open in artillery formation, and as I watched them go forward, the enemy's shrapnel was playing freely round them, but each little group pressed on until they reached the village and passed from sight. At 2 p. m. the whole of our artillery commenced intense gun fire, and all around us the field guns joined in with sharp angry barks, Avhilst the whistle, swish, and groan of shells of all calibres filled the air with noise.

On these occasions I always have an intense desire to sleepâ the din affects one in such a manner that one's eyes almost inevitably close.

Climbing to the top of the roof of my quarters I could now see columns of what looked like red smokeâ the dust of the brickstacksâ mixing with the black and white of the incessant explosions, and rising in the air.

At 2.15 the Irish Guards and Coldstream assaulted and rushed the enemy's trenches with the bayonet, and the Herts' supporting companies doubled forward in the rear waves with sand-bags, tools, and ammunition. Guardsmen could be seen chasing Germans round the brickstacks, and in a very few minutes the whole garrison were either dead or captured, whilst the attackers proceeded to consolidate.

The bootyâ machine guns, a trench mortar, stores, etc.â was sent to the rear; and now the enemy began to hate us with his guns, but it was too late, for the whole operation was completed.

The two little attacks of the preceding day had also come o0, and Lord Cavan's plans had succeeded in every particular; losses had been inflicted on the enemy, our casualties were slight, and we had got every yard we set out to win.

Our lads came back that night after their first journey across No Man's Land, laden 86 ATTACK ON THE BRICKSTACKS pt. i with the spoils of war in the shape of helmets, rifles, and bayonets, and most of them smoking German cigars.

One of our companies remained in some support trenches, and were heavily shelled. During this shelling two Herts stretcher-bearers were sent for to convey a wounded man out. As they ran down the trench a shell knocked in the parapet and half buried them both; one was wounded with a shrapnel bullet in his side, and the other in the ear. It was suggested that they should hand over their job to others, but they insisted that they should carry on, as the patient was badly wounded, and carried him out to the village, where the man died and the two gallant lads were found in a state of collapse. Both these men were awarded the Russian Medal which our Allies grant to the very brave.

Next day we were ordered up to support again, and one of our companies arrived in the Coldstream line just in time to have a shoot at a feeble counter-attack, which was driven off by the fire from our trenches.

We had not taken a major part in these operations, but had nevertheless been " blooded," and we were proud to receive a message from the G. O. C. Division addressed to the Brigadier, that

He had received with unquahfied satisfaction the report of the steady, soldier-Hke bearing under heavy fire of the 1st Battahon Hertfordshire Regiment (T. F.), both in support of the attack on February 6th, and again during the bombardment on the afternoon of the following day.

Now we worked like beavers, and concentrated our efforts on a long communication trench, which is famous in those parts as Hertford Street, and which we hope has saved many a valuable life for England.

We had advanced our position, and consequently had got ahead of the French, who joined us on the La Bassee Road; so on February 14th, they attacked on our right, to come level, and we got a good view of them as they went over. At first we thought they had captured their trench, but at the time this had not occurred, and a French officer who went through our right trenches after dark, with Captain Clive of the Grenadiers and Major Fowke of the R. E., had a surprising adventure.

They crossed the La Bassee Road and 88 ATTACK ON THE BRICKSTACKS pt. i entered the German trench, walking along until they came to some German equipment. A little further on they found a dugout lit up, and looking in, saw Germans. A sharp challenge in German by a sentry caused them to beat a hurried retreat, accompanied by bullets, and it thus transpired that the small French attacking force had been overwhelmed after entering the trench.

A subsequent French attack brought them level and included in our lines the famous mill which months after we got to know very well.

The 4th Guards Brigade, after the attack at Cuinchy, settled down to improve the Une, and everywhere we sapped forward and joined the saps, thus advancing the Hne. The Herts went into the left of the Givenchy sector, which was a very interesting part of the front, for here we were on the extreme northern edge of the high ground, and our trench line ran down what is known as the Bluff to the flat land which runs right away north.

On our left was a gap of some 600 yards between us and the La Plantin sector, which at this time was held by another brigade; there was therefore a regular crescent in the line, and to us was allotted the task of making a breastwork right out in the open in this wide stretch of No Man's Land. This was the more exciting, as the German trenches were absolutely in line with our trenches on the Givenchy front, and looking down, off our Bluff we actually commanded the top of their trenches for several miles, a fact which upsets another war theory, for it is now proved that where trenches are sufficiently traversed, enfilade firing of Infantry, at any rate, cannot turn you out.

Our plan was to build a breastwork up in the open and to go in a straight line towards the Germans on our left, the idea being ultimately to capture the German front line and thus straighten the crescent. Now to build a breastwork within a few hundred yards of the enemy is not an easy task, and very different to digging a trench, but we decided to start by making sand-bag forts with gaps between, so that in case of necessity we could occupy the forts prior to an attack, even though the breastwork was not finished.

The first night was simple, for after elaborate preparations we carried out 1,000 filled sand-bags and had a working party in No Man's Land filling others. When dawn came, therefore, fifty yards from our left there appeared a magnificent erection of brand new sand-bag work which greatly delighted us and annoyed Fritz, who proceeded to shell the fort during the day, although it was unoccupied.

The next night we proceeded to make another fort fifty yards on, and with rehefs all through the night another substantial edifice appeared at dawn.

We had now progressed 100 yards in the direction of the enemy, so he became still more savage, and we quite realised that during the next night he would probably be very busy with artillery and machine guns laid on the spot where the third fort would appear fifty yards farther on, so we decided to get our men out directly after dark, carry all our material with us, and jump 100 yards, and this artifice proved successful, for whereas our men were working all night long within 100 yards of that section of the German trench which was on our left, they were shelling and sweeping with machine guns the interval where they expected us to be.

The brigade on our left by now were making substantial progress with the breast-work which was coming forward to meet ours, and after a time we had filled all the gaps and had a continual line of breastworks, and were heartily congratulated on completing our difficult and dangerous task.

One night, another battalion, fresh out from England, was attached to us for in-struction, and so we put them on to build breastwork in No Man's Land by way of introducing them to war; and as there was a good deal of shell fire knocking about, which is rather alarming to new troops, they were, I think, rather pleased, when the German fire became intense, to be ordered back to the trenches. As it was pitch-dark and no talking was allowed, our officers and noncommissioned officers had rather a difficulty in collecting the party, all of whom had been ordered to lie flat during the shelling, and a subaltern told me a rather amusing story about how he discovered one of our sergeants haranguing a London soldier on the ground. " Get up," he said, " you lazy Cockney. Do you think I am going to stand about here all night getting you fellows in? " As the Cockney, in the darkness of the night, apparently refused to budge, the sergeant, growing emphatic, gave the offender a kick; and still finding no response, he stooped down and discovered he had been addressing a dead cow.

Another good story is told in connection with this breastwork. A battalion fresh from home took over the line, and the first night a large party was told off to carry hurdles, etc., across country to where the breastwork was being completed. There was a bright moon, and the troops in the line were not occupying the breastwork; but as the party approached they saw figures walking about on our side of the breastwork, whereupon the party lay down and opened rapid fire, and messages were sent back to say that the enemy had broken through the line. It was only an hour later that it was discovered that the imagined intruders were our own sappers waiting for the party, and they had managed to escape this murderous and enthusiastic fire by crawling along a very shallow trench to our own line on the right.

The Brigadier told me how he had heard the alarming news, and I asked him what he did? " Oh," he replied, "I mounted my servant as a sentry; but I had heard these stories so often that I was not unduly alarmed!"

During our stay in this sector we made great strides in the art of trench mortars, and by begging, borrowing, stcahng, and sometimes indenting, we succeeded in collecting quite a number of what were known as gas-pipes. They were very rough-and-ready trencli mortars: simply a circular metal tube with a couple of legs in front to make them sit up and a little hole at the bottom through which to put a fuse. Through the hole was poured a little powder and a few inches of fuse; down the tube is dropped a home-made bomb, the fuse is lit, the operators run for their lives, and suddenly there is a loud thut, and the bomb is clearly observed going high into the air until it drops in the neighbourhood of trenches, preferably German. Shortly after this there is a loud explosion, and if the shot is a lucky one, all sorts of interesting things are seen to be elevated. These primitive weapons had their disadvantages, for frequently they burst, and then, if the mortar team had not absented themselves, there was trouble. In addition to this, they called down special hate of the enemy, who would carefully mark the spot from which the mortar was fired and then concentrate a battery on the spot.

The result of this was that the mortar guns which were manned by our own men became somewhat unpopular with the Infantry, and we could only console them by reminding them how much they disliked German mortars. The moment the " thut ' of our mortar guns was heard, we could hear the enemy blowing horns and whistles, with a view to warning the garrison, who thus were able to see the direction in which our bombs were going to fall and clear out of the way. We therefore adopted new tactics, by which at a given signal we fired some twenty mortars on a one-mile front simultaneously, and in co-operation with the late Major Trefusis commanding the Irish Guards (who was promoted Brigadier-General prior to his being killed in this very sector some months later) we organised many of these mortar strafes.

About this time mining activity became more general, and we had frequent alarums and excursions in this connection. Mining activity, which is continuous on large sectors of the front, always keeps troops in the neighbourhood on tenter-hooks, and many are the reports which come from companies in the front line to the effect that the enemy can be heard working underneath them. This usually turns out to be some one digging in a deep dug-out in our own lines. The object of mining is of course to get under your enemy's trenches and to blow him, and in order to prevent this, countermining takes place. When the enemy miners are heard, we mine in their direction, and try and blow him before he blows us. It is the least spectacular form of warfare, but it demands great courage and endurance on the part of the miners, for when the enemy blows his mine, even if our shaft is not wrecked, the occupants are liable to be asphyxiated by fumes.

The first indication that you have of a mine being blown is a great rocking sensation like an earthquake, immediately after which a dull roar is heard and tons of earth are thrown into the air, forming a crater, sometimes 50 to 150 feet wide. When a mine is heard it is always an anxious moment, whilst we wonder whether the enemy has succeeded in getting under our line, although frequently he blows in No Man's Land, with a view to occupying the crater either for offensive or defensive purposes.

The side which fires the mine obviously has the great advantage in occupying the crater, as they are all prepared; and if the intrusion is too embarrassing to the defenders' trenches, a counter-attack has to be made at once in order to get possession of the crater.

As a matter of fact, in many parts of the line the Germans and ourselves each hold their own lip of the crater, and it is death to either to show themselves. In these spots hand-bombing is of course a continual attraction.

In this same sector, some months after I had left my regiment, the following incident took place. An advanced post was held by a platoon of thirty-five men, and the Germans opposite them had become very active, whereupon Lieut.- Colonel Page, my successor in command of the Herts, decided that he would withdraw the garrison temporarily whilst the enemy's work was thoroughly shelled. The garrison were accordingly withdrawn, and within five minutes the work which they had held was blown by an enemy mine.

But for this extraordinary coincidence there is little doubt that the whole garrison would have been killed.

Other corps have been less fortunate, and at times mining on both sides must have inflicted severe casualties, but on the whole, our miners always felt that they were superior to their antagonists under ground, just as the Infantry arc superior on the top.

Colonel Page, who commanded the battalion for eighteen months, was killed at St. Julian in the great attack of July 31st, 1917.

On February 10th, at 4.30 a. m. the brigade was in reserve for the offensive at Neuve Chapelle. In order to arrive at our rendezvous we left Bethune at about 2 a. m. and marched to Le Preol, where we rested beside La Bassec Canal. Just as we were arriving at this spot we could hear the roar of the guns as the intense bombardment heralded the attack. The sound was just like continuous thunder, and one could not help contrastingâ for war is all contrastsâ the peaceful spot where we settled down to wait with the inferno which was raging a few miles off.

Whilst we were waiting and expecting every moment to be ordered to take our sharc in the proceedings, various scraps of news came through to us, and we heard of the great success of the original attack on the line and of prisoners being marched to the rear, and we realised that a turning point had come in the war, for up to now neither side had really succeeded in storming any considerable line of trenches.

At Neuve Chapelle the tactics of Cuinchy were adopted on a larger scale, viz. the surprise attack after an intense concentrated bombardment; but once again the British Army was to learn the lesson of the extraordinary power of machine guns well placed. During the main attack at Neuve Chapelle our division was making a subsidiary attack on Givenchy, and there the 1st 60th, 2nd South Staffords, and the 1st King's made a very gallant attempt with small artillery support to capture the Bluff and the high ground just north of the La Bassee Canal. Four times the South Staff ords entered the German front trench, but foiu' times were driven out by machine guns. The King's reached the German wire, which they could not penetrate, and the 60th, who entered the German trench in the only place where the wire was cut, could not maintain their hold. At night on the first day of Neuve Chapelle wc marched back again to billets, and the next day marched to Givenchy, where we relieved the sorely tried 6th Brigade, whilst the attack, away on our left, progressed a little farther.

It is never a cheery job taking over trenches from battalions which have just received a knock; and besides being somewhat heavily shelled, we were busily engaged after dark trying to rescue wounded in No Man's Land; and three nights after the attack one of our company sergeant-majors went out to the German wire and brought back on his back a wounded corporal of the K. R. R. The next night we succeeded in bringing in two more wounded men of the same corps who had lain out there four days and four nights.

The net result of Neuve Chapelle was, that the 1st Army made the biggest bag of prisoners since the war of position had started, and had shown that with careful artillery preparation the German front system, at any rate, could be carried. We had also learnt once again in this subsidiary attack that little can be gained by attacking an enemy position whilst the wire remains intact.

With the drying of the ground work proceeded apace, and we very soon turned the Cuinchy and Givenchy sectors into a really first-class system of trenches, and our casualties, which had been heavy when we first entered the line, were rapidly decreasing as we deepened, traversed, and perfected oiir line. My head-quarters for three weeks were at a famous spot known as Windy Corner, in rear of Givenchy, and two or three times a day the enemy artillery searched the village. In the farm next to our head-quarters an unlucky shell pitched right in the doorway, mortally wounding four men, and another shell penetrated our roof, but on the whole we were extremely lucky, especially as in one day, March 19th, the enemy fired no less than 2,000 heavy shells in our neighbourhood, a large proportion of which fell around the ruins of Givenchy Church.

During the afternoon I was walking up to the line and watching German 8-inch shells bursting on Givenchy, sending up clouds of brick-dust and hurling their debris considerable distances, when I heard one shell coming towards the church, which was a quarter of a mile from where I stood, and was astonished, instead of hearing it burst,, to hear a terrific humming noise and to see the shell coming straight in my direction. As I lay flat on the ground it came buzzing like an enormous bee, and fell with a thud in the ground twenty yards from where I lay.

This was a " dud" shell which had pitched on the hill at Givenchy and had ricochetted in my direction, but happily, being a " dud " it did not explode when it reached my neighbourhood, to my intense relief.

The normal trench life proceeded, and a few yards from my house was the British cemetery which, when we first came, contained only a dozen graves, but which, before we left those parts, stretched over an acre of ground. Every day the chaplain would come up and men of different regiments would be reverently conveyed to their graves, which were beautifully kept and marked with various descriptions of wooden crosses and little metal plates attached, with the name, number, and regiment clearly marked thereon. These cemeteries are eventually wired round, and the whole work is now carried out with great care.

Every day, these spring mornings, aeroplanes would circle overhead, and sentries were posted at intervals to warn the men billeted in the villages when a German was in the heavens. Daily you could see our aeroplanes going far over the German lines, hunted all the way by what looked like little white puffs of smokeâ in reality, bursting shrapnelâ and frequently you could see a plane with fifty white puffs stretching out behind it where the wind had not yet dispersed the smoke of the bursting shrapnel.

Now the ordinary Infantry man knows that a German shell is not intended for him, and consequently he thinks it is merely bad luck when they pitch in his direction; but for the airman it is different, for every one of those innocent puffs means 200 shrapnel bullets intended for him individually, and therein lies the great difference in the outlook of the man in the air as opposed to the man on the ground.

It is a remarkable thing, when frequently thousands of shells are fired into the air in the course of the day, that there are not many casualties as a result of the falling fragments. The pieces come down with a humming noise, and strange as it may seem, these hummings are regarded with great contempt by every one who hears them. In reality, of course, they are coming down about the same pace as the shell goes up, so that if they do hit you, you are likely to know all about it. In all my long time in the trenches I only saw one mishap of this description, and that was when we were lazily sitting outside a billet a mile behind the line in the sun, and watching one of our planes circling over the enemy's trenches. We could hear distant enemy rifle fire aimed against the plane, and a man in my regiment was walking along the road towards us when all of a sudden he fell. It transpired that a bullet had entered the nape of his neck and gone right through his body and out at his heel, and he died as the result of his wounds. This, however, was an exceptional case, and I am reminded of the philosophy of a private in my company when I first went to France, who told me that " there was far more air about than lead." We decided, however, to make the life of the German airman as uncomfortable as possible, and so whenever he came low over our lines we opened rapid fire upon him, but although this was very uncomfortable for the airman, I must confess that beyond keeping him up high I never saw damage inflicted upon him; the only time that I saw an airman forced to descend by fire from trenches was when a Lewis gun got in a lucky shot and forced him to descend behind the German lines.

Whilst we were in the Givenchy sector we were pestered by German field artillery, which was very active. The guns have a low trajectory, and if you are being fired at, and happen to be in the way, you do not hear them coming, " whizâ bang " being heard almost simultaneously, and then you are lucky if you are only covered with earth. These shells do remarkably little harm, although sometimes a direct hit on the parapet with percussion will play mischief, and then men get buried. On one occasion in this tour I was walking round a traverse, and a shell burst in the next bay. A scared man ran round the traverse, and I asked him if any one was hurt? " Bill may be," he said, but Bill could not be found, so I gave the order to dig, and we dug Bill out just in time, and respiration brought him back to life and hope.

Shrapnel shows discrimination. I was once walking up a trench between two men much shorter than myself when a shell burst straight in front of us, and both ny attendants were hit, whilst I went unscathed.

Early in INIay there were whisperings of Uvehness in Flanders, and subtle rumour made the round of trench and billet. These rumours usually come from England, where somebody's wife has heard that a big push is coming off, and as she, in confidence, invariably tells somebody else's wife, eventually in spite of the imperative necessity of secrecy, these rumours are spread all through England and thence to France.

On May Gth, the whole of the 4th Guards Brigade was in line holding from the La Bassee Road to Lc Plantin, and on May 8th, at 4.45 a. m., the British artillery commenced a great bombardment on our left, which was taken up by the French artillery on our right.

I went to the top of a high building, and there I could see the whole of the ground between Givenchy and Ncuve Chapelle where the attack was to take place.

Hundreds of shells could be seen bursting along the German line every minute, and the whole world seemed to vibrate with the sounds of hell. Immediately to our right the French " 75 " guns were adding their music, " thud, thud, thud, thud " in quick succession, until all the south was thudding its chorus.

Just before the bombardment commenced in the dim light of dawn a British aeroplane was seen returning over the lines, flying low under fire, when, to the horror of all our men, it burst into flames and dived to earth in No Man's Land, and all those who look for signs and portents wagged their heads.

At 5.40 a. m. the attack commenced, and British and French left their trenches to the north and south of us respectively. The British attack had the effect of a right wheel, and the French a left wheel, and we were the first pivot of each attack, and stood firm whilst we hoped the attacks would progress so as to envelop La Bassee opposite us.

Directly the attack began, all our five battalions opened rapid fire on the German trenches, the idea being to prevent the machine guns opposite us bringing flanking 110 THE BATTLE OF FESTUBERT pt. i fire to bear on the attackers and to hold the enemy reserves opposite us.

From the Herts trenches the French bayonets could be seen glittering in the sun as their long waves of attackers advanced, and then we longed for news, which seems to take ages to filter through on such occasions.

Soon we heard that the attack immediately on our left by the 1st Division had been held up by wire, but that the 4th Corps away to the north was progressing well, and the French were getting on.

Reports now came through of German troops concentrating at La Bassee and Violaines opposite us, and remembering the passion of the enemy for attacking at the junction of the French and British armies, we ardently prayed for a counter-attack, which never came. In the afternoon we learnt that the French had captured trenches opposite Loos, andâ a great triumphâ they had wrested from the Llun the vital spur of Notre Dame de Lorette. The British 1st Division, we heard, had tried again, but once more the wire had defeated them.

We were in a kind of backwater where all was calm, whilst the rushing torrents of war were surging to either side of us, and so we sat warming ourselves in the sun.

just as if we were in some land of peace whilst thousands of men were fighting and dying within a mile or so on either side of us. Not a shell was fired at us, and as night descended we Hstened to the distant roar, and each man wondered, "Are we too for it?"

We soon heard, for on May 13th we were reheved by the 1 st Division, and the Camerons took over the hne held by the Herts. The 1st Brigade had been very badly mauled in their attacks, and had left many gallant Highlanders behind; and as we knew that we were going to march to that same place from whence they came, their news was not too cheery.

We marched to Le Touret, where we lay down in a field which was allotted to us for a bivouac. The next day we were given buildings for billets, which pleased us as the nights were cold, and we then heard that the attack of the previous Sunday, which had failed, was to be rcattempted. And so the usual joke went round. "They 'ad ter send for us Guards," says a Hertfordshire Territorial. " Whenever there's a job as no one else can tackle, they wires for the blooming old 2nd Division. Serves the 'Uns right, says I."

This was Saturday, May 14th, and for us nothing doing, so I rode away to the rear, where the harsh bark of the guns becomes a muffled boom; there where the sun poured out its joyous warmth for the fields and the trees to bathe in, where birds sing and children play.

So we rode through villages and over fields, a friend and I, and we might have been away back in Hertfordshire.

Guardsmen were billeted in several of the villages, and cheering could be heard as terrific games of football progressed. What a strange race we are! Look at those hulking giant babies, rushing for goal whilst comrades cheer; and to-morrow they will rush again, when all will play, and none will be spectators. Then, too, men will fall in the mudâ yes, men will fall in the mud.

Back to Le Touret, and what a different scene! From dusk until 10.30 p. m. the troops who were to attack early on the morrow marched along the main road past our little cottage. It is good to be a Briton when British troops march to the attack. No band here; no cheering crowds; but 114 THE EDGE OF THE BATTLE pt. i song: the kind of songs we often hear whcn troops at night are marching hack to rest, but the singing is less harsh â there is more music, or so it seems. They see us watching them go by, and there is just a touch of swagger, just a half smile, for they know that the spectators are asking themselves how many of the songsters will come back by that road; they know in this hour they are British. That is why they swagger, and that is why they sing and smile.

More troops and moreâ English, Scottish, AVelsh, and Irishâ on they go; and now night, with its quiet hours, is here, and so singing must stop or the enemy will shell the roads.

We heard quips and jokes, and more battalions move by with the same unequalled look of the British regular army. Many battalions marched by who had caught it at Mons, at Le Cateau and the Aisne, who had got it in the neck at Ypres, who knew their modern war; but although there were many there fresh from the depots, there were none who had failed to win the spirit of the great dead, who in dying had stopped the barbarian hordes and saved Calais, Havre, and perhaps the world.

The 4th Guards Brigade were now warned as Corps Reserve, and at 11.30 p. m. the attack commenced, and messages came through to say that the 5th and 6th Brigades, both of our division, had gained ground and captured trenches.

At 2.45 a. m. the terrific noise of our guns hailed a second attack, and I ran outside, to see the heavens splashed with what looked like continuous lightning, whilst field guns cracked and barked their unearthly chorus and heavies moaned and purred their way over our heads from miles behind; then scores of German star shells lit the land, and great events we knew were happening.

At 3.25, suddenly sprays of white stars proclaimed the fact that the 7th Division had gained their objective on the right, and we knew it was time for breakfast, for we were veterans enough now to remember that no man can fight on an empty stomach, and soon the whole battalion was drawing on the cookers.

A disturbed night this, which is a pity, for who can tell if there is sleep for the Herts for the, next few days?

A day of sensation it turned out, for soon our road was a continuous picture of interest. Artillery limbers trotting up with ammuni- 116 THE EDGE OF THE BATTLE pt. i tion, and empty limbers with sweating horses galloping back for more; Red Cross motors moving down the road gently with their burdens; groups of wounded men walking back chaffing and joking; this one with a blood-stained bandage round his head, another with his coat ripped open and shoulder bound; here is one limping between two bandaged comrades; there is a lad, very young and very pale, but he waves a German helmet and laughsâ then faints beside the road.

Shells begin to crack in the neighbourhood, but nobody seems disturbed, least of all a fair-haired boy who has a word for all, as they limp to Blighty. All guess his identity, and as they pass on we hear them say, "Some Prince, that!"

Now we see a surging crowd of Tommies rush into the road, and there round the corner come grey figures, prisoners to join the procession on the highway. They pass, ten or twenty at a time, with two or three Tommies with fixed bayonets, who look as if they have suddenly heard that some distant aunt had left them fortunes.

One does not expect prisoners to look pleased, but it is not a good type of face this. Some of them, it is true, are better, but most have the look of the man in the dockâ the man who before you have heard the evidence possesses the look of guilt.

Be careful, my friends, in believing that the Kaiser alone is bad, for the vast majority of these Prussians possess the face of a brute.

We now heard that Canadians were expected to arrive in the area, and I walked along the road to meet them. So far Canadians had not come our way, and we had only heard the fine story of how they stood firm in the great gas attack at Ypres.

Soon the head of a column comes in view, the Canadian Highland Brigade, and here they are, the cousins from over the pond who have come thousands of miles to do their bit. There I recognise, riding at the head of their men, bankers and merchants of Toronto, Real Estate agents and others who have forgotten all that dollars mean, left the wheat pits and the town plots, who have forsaken the building of a nation to save the fabric of Empire. On they came, hundreds and thousands, marching along with a swing and the look of men who have " been there." Fine fellows these, and it is something to know that if we bite the dust the Canadians will be behind us to carry on.

Lord Cavan calls a hurried conference of commanding officers at the Herts head-quarters, and orders are given that the Grenadiers and Irish Guards will take over the captured German trenches, the Herts will be in support, and the 2nd and 3rd Coldstream in reserve. The brigade was to attack the line Ferme Coeur D'Avoigneâ Quinque Rue. We fell out by the side of the road in Le Touret and waited for the Grenadiers and Irish to pass.

Soon they came, marching at that stately stride which denotes the Guards, and we throw and catch cheery words from our comrades of many months as they swing by, looking the embodiment of all that is perfect in the fighting man. Sometimes, Londoners, you may wonder at all the little tricks of drill and footwork as you watch the Guards in Birdcage Walk, and when you see the harsh discipline sometimes you ask, is it not overdone? No, a thousand times no, for if you saw your pipe clayed polished Guards in the field you would know that it is just that discipline which makes the 120 " THE GUARDS ARE FOR IT " pt. i supreme fighting man who is the pride of your army.

Again we ask the question, How many of these great cheery giants will come out of the crucible? and almost we forget that we, too, are part of the show when we see these friends of ours marching to the end of the world.

The last of the Irish are passing; a whistle blows, and the Herts fall in; a second whistle, and every rifle is sloped; a third, and the whole battalion steps out in column, joining up with that very gallant company on the roadâ the long, long road to the Rhine.

Soon we leave the road for the fields, as German woolies (5 9 high-explosive shrapnel) are cracking over our heads like last trumps, so we move quickly into artillery formation as the march continues.

We halt at last in some support trenches, and here we are to wait for orders. There had been lots of rain, and our trenches were nothing but muddy ditches; and now the rain came down in torrents as we tried to settle down to rest; but if you attempted to lie on the ground you sunk into two inches of watery mud, so there was nothing for it but to cut out little seats, and thus we waited for night and sat sleepless whilst the torrent poured on us till dawn, and we listened for news from the front.

The plan was that the Irish Guards should make a frontal attack on the farm Coeur D'Avoigne, the Grenadiers on their right taking the farm in flank. One company of the Herts was ordered to attack on the left of the Irish Guards, and the remaining three companies to be ready to support either of the attacking battalions.

The attack intended originally for dawn was postponed until 9 a. m., and then to 4.30 p. m. Meanwhile our attacking company moved up just in rear of the Irish Guards, and we marched up behind breastworks just in rear of them. All day the Germans shelled the trenches with heavies, and when I went to see our forward company they were sitting with very little cover whilst shells were falling with loud crumps all round them, but just not on them. Whilst I had a hurried conversation with the company commander a shell exploded in a cottage 200 yards away, and a mass of black smoke, mingled with red brick-dust, belched upwards, and crash in all directions went 122 " THE GUARDS ARE FOR IT " pt. i bricks, timber, and earth. When the dust cleared there was no cottage left.

The Canadians now came up behind us, and at 4.20 p. m. a ten minutes' bombardment of intense character, a terrific reply from the Germans, and then the attack was launched. I moved up to see what was happening, and streams of wounded Irish Guardsmen began to trail backâ a sickening sight for supporting troopsâ and I found myself up in our old salient of Christmas, in ground I knew. The noise was now terrific, so that there might have been a thousand devils loose in the air, when a messenger of the Irish Guards rushed up to me and asked if I had seen the commanding officer. " No," I replied.

"Then, sir," he said, "I report to you. All our officers are hit, and I have been sent back here to report for orders."

"How far have you advanced? " I queried.

"Three hundred yards from behind the German trench, and absolutely held up by machine guns."

I could not find Major Trefusis the CO., and feared he was hit, so I decided to reinforce with one company, which happened to be my old company from my native town, and in twenty minutes they appeared and I sent them over the top. Every man I knew well as they came by me in the trench whilst Irish Guards were filtering back to the dressing station, bleeding and reeling, and Irish Guards were lying dead across the bottom of the trench, but not a man of ours faltered, and many a joke was cracked for my edification as they formed up. Then over they went, and machine gun bullets began to tap, tap, tap, around.

Now I was in the old German trench, and there to my delight I found Trefusisâ bravest of soulsâ alive, cool, and deliberate, so we discussed the situation, and I told him that I had been ordered to relieve his battalion after dark.

There, out in front of us, was the khaki line all lying flat and gradually digging in on the ground as they lay.

We now made plans for the relief, and I got back to the salient where my headquarters were by now established. Herts wounded were beginning to come back, and on a stretcher I espied a man who had served under me many years in time of peace. He was the wag of the company, and his waggishness led several times to slight 124 " THE GUARDS ARE FOR IT " pt. i insubordination, and he had appeared before me at orderly room.

Now, as he lay face down on the stretcher and saw me, a roguish look entered his eyes and his pale face lit up as he said, "Well, sir, I shan't worry you any more; that will be a relief to you at orderly room." I saw he was in frightful pain, and I confess to a prayer that he might be spared to cause me endless orderly rooms. I remembered that half an hour before I had heard him cheering on his mates with ridiculous jokes as he climbed over the top.

It is instructive to see how the bad boys of the family often shine in warâ this is only one good reason why we should not judge too freely when we thank God we are not as other men.

The net result of the attack was that the Grenadiers, Irish Guards, and our company of Herts had advanced 300 yards beyond the German trenches, where further progress was hopeless as the ground in front was a glacis which was swept by machine gun fire.

Our company on the left had, with a machine gun of the Irish Guards, progressed farthest; and Major Page of the Herts, with twenty men, actually got on about 200 yards fartherâ quite close to the objective; but finding himself in the air and isolated, came back in line with the advanced attackers when it was clear that no support could reach him.

The remnants of the attackers, reinforced by two more Herts platoons, dug in in the open in front of the enemy, and refused to budge an inch as they gradually burrowed their way underground.

Directly dark came I went out with two fresh companies and sited the new Hne, and got them to work with pick and shovel. Meanwhile the battlefield had to be cleared. Dead and wounded were lying about all over the ground.

All night long our stretcher bearers and volunteers from the spare companies were searching for wounded, and here a voice calling in the night and there a groan guided the good Samaritans who laboured on through the long hours until every single wounded man had been conveyed back to safety. Meanwhile the digging went on unceasingly in reliefs, because we knew that unless we could dig in by dawn, hell was in store for us. Just as dawn was coming the protecting screen was brought in, and the trench was down, all along the 350-yards front, to an average depth of four feet, and magnificently traversed.

It was a grand piece of work by men who had had no sleep for two days and nights, who had been drenched to the skin and been under incessant shell fire; and well it was, for, but for that great night's work, few would have survived the shelling which dawn was to bring.

All that day the new trench was shelled by 5 9 high explosives, and for hours the deafening crack went on as the green and white fumes burst and rolled away in woolly clouds.

We were all fatigued, and any moment we expected a counter-attack, till at last the hour approached for our relief by the 2nd Coldstream at dusk. As it got dark, however, the Germans redoubled their efforts, and such was the barrage that for over two hours the Coldstream had to wait before they could approach the trenches.

A corporal coming out from the front line, dazed and shaken, told how he was the last of his company, but I found out that high explosives had wiped out fourteen men to his right and left, and he had crawled back, hardly knowing where he was or what had happened.

That day's shelling cost us sixty casualties in our new trench, and with these added to our losses of the day before, we left the line with the loss of six officers and 124 other ranks, of whom twenty-two were killed. During the last twenty- four hours our stretcher bearers had dressed no less than 300 wounded men of our own and the Irish, and carried more than 100 stretcher cases a mile back to the dressing station. Those who know can realise the kind of ground we had to work in, pitted with craters and oozing with mud, and will I think agree that this is no mean feat.

The fatigue of that night was great. I had a sprained ankle, and could hardly keep awake on my horse as I rode back, and how much more my men must have suffered from exhaustion I can only guess.

We were a very weary crowd on relief, but we were proud, for, as our general told us later, we had done all that soldiers could do. We had advanced our line, we had dug in in face of the enemy in daylight, and we had stayed there under a shelling which had tested to top strain the sticking power of human beings.

The following day we marched to Bethune, and the next to Labeuvriere, a charming village with many trees all green with early foliage, a brook to bathe in, and woods through which to roam at will and forget. Our quarters were in a delightful old convent with a shaded garden, where we spread ourselves lengthwise on the lawn and got our news of how the Canadians carried on in the land we had left.

A church parade and complimentary words from Major-General Home, commanding the division, battalion drills and practising wood fighting, with alfresco concerts in the convent garden at nightâ all tended to bring us back to fighting form. Give Tommy pleasant surroundings, and he soon recovers from any ordeal.

After a delightful rest the brigade marched to Noeux les Mines, an inhabited mining village, where we took over from the French reserves. I had a nice little house for my head-quarters, and had just settled down in a deck-chair on the equally nice garden when a German shell took a piece out of the garden wall. It w as not meant for the garden, but for the cross-roads 100 yards beyond, so it was no good worryingâ probably an enemy aeroplane had seen the brigade on the march. After that the Bochc lengthened, and we were less disturbed.

St. Andrew's Day demanded a banquet of Old Etonians, and some sixty of the old school in the brigade sat down to a magnificent spread in the Hotel de Ville. Our Brigadier and all five commanding officers were there to sing the old songs which Lord Cavan led with a will, and after dinner the subalterns danced together whilst we old gentlemen wended our way home to our billets.

From Noeux les Mines we marched to Annequin, and the brigade took over the line south of the La Bassee road; and here we advanced the whole line by digging forward so that No Man's Land by Hohenzouern redoubt was reduced by a hundred yards.

Soon we had what was for us, sad news, that Lord Cavan, under whom we had served since we came to France, was off to command a division. He was succeeded in command of the brigade by Colonel Geoffrey Fielding, who was an old friend, as he had commanded the 3rd Coldstream all these months.

Back we went to the Givenchy line again, and here we were busily engaged in making breastworks in front of Le Plantin, and for some time the 2nd Division remained in these parts improving the line.

Resting at Le Quesnoy we had a grand sermon one day from the Bishop of Khartoum. Bishop Gwynne, who looks like " John

Bull," has a way with soldiers which counts, and the happy knack of making men proud of the part they are playing, and before he has finished preaching you feel that not only are you going to win the war for right against wrong, but that you are all eventually going home to turn England into a better, happier place than it has ever been â surely this must be an influence for good.

We were getting veiy expert in the use of hand grenades, and a large proportion of the battahon had learnt the use of the bombs which were now handed out. Our bombers were the heroes of the battalion, and some of them became quite famous for their skill.

Bombing was no joke in the early days, as many accidents occurred and casualties were unhappily frequent, because no perfect bomb had been invented. Two gallant young Guards officers, who were the bombing instructors of the brigade, had lost their lives during instruction. One of them was killed by a bomb exploding in his pupil's hand not a hundred yards from where I stood.

These accidents were a great worry, as the moral effect was bad, but I am glad to say that officers were always ready to take a class within an hour of a fatal accident, and the work was carried on.

When we started we used jam tins, and as the bomb was of local manufacture, the dangers were always great; one thing, however, was clear, and that was that trenches had recently been lost by the enemy bombing our people out, and the only way to beat bombs was by bombs, so we all put our minds to this matter.

The " Batty " bomb and the " Ball " bombs were now the fashion: the Batty, a light bomb which was fairly safe if properly charged; the Ball bomb, a round, heavy bomb which was ignited by striking on a bracelet like a safety match, a splendid contrivance so long as it did not rain, as events proved in days to come.

We had throwing competitions, and very soon the men became as keen to win the long distance or the accuracy competition as they were at other games of skill and strength.

We were lucky in these days in having Bethune, a town of considerable size, for our rest place. The enemy's shells had not up to this time done any very disastrous damage, and with its shops and market it was a great change to the men after coming out of the line. There was a big theatre here, which I believe is no longer in use, but we used to have numerous concerts therein, and regiments would vie with each other in trying to put on the best show.

There was also an hotel where you could get quite a good meal, and a cafe where officers adjourned to about 5.30 p. m. for champagne cocktails; but best of all, there were large numbers of comfortable houses where you could feel civilised, sleep between sheets, and really pretend that all sorts of things had never happened. Amongst these houses was a fine chateau where an old lady and her daughters continued to live in spite of frequent bombardments, and the dower-house in the same grounds was much sought after as a battahon head-quarters.

On occasion, this grande dame lent her own dining-room for dinner parties, and here I remember dining with the Irish Guards off beautiful plate and in great luxury provided by the hostess. The Prince of Wales was present; also Sir Charles Munro the Corps commander, and other generals, sitting round a table which was beautifully decorated with flowers, and this within four hours of our coming out of muddy trenches.

Now, however, came a sad time for the Herts, for we learnt that the Guards Division was to be formed, and so we were to leave our comrades with whom we had fought since early in November 1914, and who had given us such a royal welcome and never ceased to make us feel we were of themselves.

General Fielding, the Brigadier, afterwards the distinguished conmiander of the Guards Division, bade us farewell at Le Quesnoy, anrf loh us things which made us proud, ar d paid us a tribute that was so sincerely uttered that we knew that we had really reached our aim â " to be regarded as amongst the equals of the best of the British Army."

A farewell dinner was given by the officers of the Grenadiers to the Divisional Staff, and I was honoured by an invitation. These partings are sad, but I told the Grenadiers that I supposed the Herts would now have to try and raise the standard of some other brigade, wherefore I soon found myself being shouted down, so we parted the best of friends before I had read them my complete lecture on how soldiers on active service should comport themselves!

On August 19th the Guards marched away. The route was lined by detachments of all the other battalions in the division, but to the Herts were given the place of honour, and a full company lined the route where General Home took the salute.

Headed by the brass band of the 2nd Division, down the road they marched, and our lads cheered each battalion as they came along, until the end of the column had gone by and the grandest panorama of humanity had passed before our eyes.

What would happen to us? Our fate was soon decreed, and to our joy we were to stay in the 2nd Division as part of the famous 6th Brigade. We received a very cordial welcome from Brigadier-General Daly, who told us that if we came near our reputation, he would be more than pleased.

We soon found oui-selves astride the La Bassee Road, and occupying the trench round the old mill which we had seen the French capture months before. This sector, and those north and south, are the scenes of great mine fighting; in fact, most of this front for about a mile is nothing but huge mine craters.

This broken ground made a great obstacle for an attacking force, as we were later to find; and, in addition, some of the craters, notably Etna and Vesuvius south of the road, were held on either lip by the opposing forces.

As the enemy was frequently patrolling these craters, and our patrols were often out, some very pretty scraps with bombs used to take place.

To command a crater you have to fortify the near lip before the enemy has succeeded in fortifying his Hp, otherwise you cannot Hve comfortably in occupation; but once you have got a protected loop-hole established which commands the crater, then you ought to be able to shoot any one who tries to fortify opposite. To be quite restful, of course, where you can you capture the whole crater, but this is not always possible in No Man's Land, where the trenches are close.

Wlien we took over the Etna line south of the road, the battalion we relieved had commanded the crater until that morning, when at dawn a German sniper, firing over the top of his lip, succeeded in shooting the sentry through the iron loop-hole. As the sentry was killed, the enemy thus got time to erect a loop-hole and to command the crater, and so it was w hen we came in.

That night a free exchange of bombs took place, nmny hundreds being thrown before the fight finished, and both sides were convinced that the crater could not be held.

A few days later I was visiting the left of our line when I was nearly knocked off my feet by a mine explosion quite close, and found myself in a shower bath of earth. On inspection we found that Boche had "blown " in No Man's Land opposite the battalion just on our left, and as the crater was some way from both lines, neither side tried to occupy. Two days after we left this line a mine was blown under the front trench, and our successors had many casualties.

All along this front we were pestered by German Minenwerfers and other trench mortars. There was one particularly obnoxious visitor, known as Silver King, who flew silently through the air with the appearance of a silver torpedo, and when he exploded great damage resulted and large sections of the trench were blown in; in addition, other large bombs were fired at us continually, and as the explosions were terrific and the ground shook for hundreds of yards, sleep was rendered almost impossible.

As I dislike disturbed nights, I decided to enlist the help of the gunners to strafe these nuisances, and so we put on about a dozen spotters whose sole duty was to mark down from different angles the exact spot from which the smoke was seen by day or the flash by night.

We managed to bring our co-operation to such a fine art that we had special wires laid, and the gunners so thoroughly entered into the sport that they had men standing by; then, as Minnie opened her lips to fire, the code word was sent, and before she had exploded, four field howitzer shells were on voyage to sit on her. Minnie would therefore explode with her mighty crash, and within about ten seconds, crash, crash, crash, crash went the howitzers, exploding their shells all round her lair. The moral of the troops rapidly improved, and Minnie spotting became a joy.

After a day or two of this treatment, enemy Minnie was silenced, and so great became the Minnie strafe that tiger-hunting gunners from strange divisions used to come to my head-quarters to ask if they might join in. This was most improper, but most successful, and the field artillery also cooperated. What happened we do not know, but I can guess that either we knocked them out with direct hits or else the Hun infantry, who shared our vigorous hate, informed the Minnie people that if they fired again, German bayonets would for ever silence them. Be that as it may, we beat them, and were no more worried.

Ourallection for the gunners now deepened.

and we learnt the art of complete co-operation between the two arms.

Apropos of trench mortars, I may mention that one day we were visited by a distinguished company of " Brass Hats," as in these times there were rumours of wars and future attacks, and they had come to spy out the land. I was conducting this distinguished company along a trench when a whistle caused me to look up, and there, in full flight I espied a big bomb coming straight in our direction. I called out! "Bomb over," and began the usual cat dance which decides behind which traverse you are going to shelter, when, to my horror, I saw all my generals and staff prone on the floor, and the bomb racing surely towards us; but by the mercy of Heaven it exploded prematurely in the air, so stretcher bearers were not required, and I breathed again.

The natural inclination when a bomb comes over is to hide like a partridge from a hawk, but before you have lived long in bomb land, you learn to watch him very carefully on tip-toes, and if you know his ways you can invariably dodge him, unless he happens to be Silver King or some other speedy gent of that same breed.

All is bustle, digging proceeds day and night, and all ranks who are not digging are carrying materials, rations, bombs, and other necessary articles to forward dumps;

mothers, grandmothers, and other ladies of weight and dignity are coyly hiding their beauty behind; lighter guns and howitzers are collecting souvenirs for the Germans, and a mighty array of shells is appearing, whilst all men are glad that now at last we have the " stuff " to make a great offensive. The 2nd Division is on the extreme left of the push, with the 5th Brigade north of the La Bass e Canal at Givenchy, the 6th Brigade at Cuinchy, and the 19th Brigade on the right just south of the La Bassee-Bethune road; on their right again, the remainder of the 1st Corps (Gough's); and on their right again, the 4th Corps (Raw-linson's).

146 THE BLOODY FIELD OF LOOS pt. i

This is the first prolonged bombardment we have given the Huns, for the simple reason that this is the first time we have had the shells; and now for four days and nights we shell their lines, the villages behind, and the roads by which the food is conveyed to the enemy trenches. All day long the field guns, firing low over our trenches, rake the German wire; and all night long machine guns crackle as they sweep it to prevent repair of the gaps.

Our guns are taken from us for the centre of the push, and new artillery from England comes to try and learn wire cutting. A gallant scout of the Herts the night before the attack went along the whole of the German wire on our front, and reported that it was intact, with only one small gap.

This should have dismayed us, but we were told that our gas would be so effective that we would merely walk through the wire at our leisure.

At 5.40 a. m., on September 25th, we loosed gas upon the enemy. The wind, which was favourable in Loos and Vermelles, was, unhappily, unfavourableâ or Hun-favourable as our men would sayâ opposite us, and the result was that the gas of the brigade on our right drifted down in our direction, whilst ours blew towards the 5th Brigade; and although we were equipped with helmets, all prepared, this event was not conducive to a good start in the attack. The 6th Brigade were attacking, with the Kings and the South Staffords in the front line, the Herts and 1st Berks in support, and the 1st K. R. R. and 5th Liverpools in reserve; and at 6.30, as the gas lifted, over went the leading companies of the attacking battalions, whilst the supporting battalions were all moving up to the front system. The 6th Brigade were never able to penetrate the wire, and, what is more, the enemy, who were expecting the attack, opened a murderous machine gun fire, so much so, that of the leading company of the Kings in front of us, only the captainâ gallant Goffâ reached the German wire; and on getting there he turned round to find himself alone, the remainder of his leading platoon having been wiped out. He thereupon came back and, miraculous to narrate, reached our lines in safety. He w as the only officer who had remained with the 1st Kings from the start, and later, unhappily, was killed whilst leading his battalion on the Somme.

Meanwhile, the 5th Brigade on our left 148 THE BLOODY FIELD OF LOOS pt. i had made a considerable advance, although the 19th Brigade on our right had been held up with heavy losses. The remainder of the 1st Corps, however, and the 4th Corps made fine progress, capturing the German front system early in the day, and, later, the whole of the town of Loos and a considerable track of country beyond.

Our attack on the La Bassee Road having failed, we were told for that day to desist from further attempts, whereupon I betook myself to the top of a house at Bradell Point, where, with my telescope, I had a wonderful view of the advance. Quite early I was presented with the magnificent spectacle of a battery of horse artillery galloping forward past the old trenches, and where I was it looked as if the battery could not live, for shells were bursting all round them; but I suddenly saw them swing round and, in spite of riderless horses tearing wildly over the country, in about a minute I saw the flash of each gun, and I knew that the whole battery was in action. Then we could see Infantry going forward in artillery formation, whilst others were digging like fury on the high ground east of Loos, and we saw large numbers of prisoners coming back.

CH. xxviii A VOICE IN THE NIGHT 149

During that night we sent up large parties of men to assist the Kings in bringing in their casualties, and all night long they worked with a will and assisted in bringing in some scores of wounded men.

We of the Herts had been fortunate that day, for in spite of the very heavy barrage as we were reinforcing, we had hardly any casualties to report by evening.

On the 26th we were ordered to relieve the Kings in the front line.

I visited the trenches that night, and all was wonderfully calm in our sector after the fury of the preceding forty-eight hours, but jast as I was concluding my round, some silly fellow from the next battalion shouled in a very loud voice, as if he was leading an attack: " Come on, chaps! " whereupon the Boche properly got the " wind up," thinking that another attack had just started against him, and we cursed our witty friend, finding ourselves for half an hour in a perfect tornado of shells and mortars. The Germans had evidently wired through S. O. S., and were loosing coloured lights into the heavens, with the result that within 100 yards of where I crouched, in one minute there was something like 130 high-explosive shells and mortar bombs bursting. The 150 THE BLOODY FIELD OF LOOS pt. i air was thick with fumes and dust, and the wonderful thing is, that in spite of such volcanic gun and mortar fire, we only had one man buried and one slightly wounded.

The next morning further news came in of the big fight, and we realised that substantial gains had been made by our army and tlie French, but the British Infantry, which we had seen so gallantly advance as far as the village of Ilaisnes, had been forced to retire as the troops on their flanks had been held up.

Looking from my observation post I had a wonderful view of tlie famous slag heap, Fosse 8. In the first attack the British had managed to get round this great coal dump, which was hundreds of yards long, very steep, and with a flat surface at the top, forming a sort of Gibraltar standing up in the middle of otherwise flat country; but, unliappily, they were unable to maintain themselves against very strong counter-attacks. This day, therefore, our troops again attacked, and I could see khaki figures swarming right up the steep banks of the fosse; and then advancing at a double across the flat surface at the top, half the fosse was theirs, when a terrific barrage of enemy artillery opened and the attackers gradually faded away under a terrible concentrated fire. About an hour later the scene was reversed, and grey figures swarmed along that fatal surface. Immediately our guns came into action and hundreds of the grey figures were seen to fall, the attack absolutely withering up under our barrage. In this last attack the shooting of the artillery was indeed wonderful, and within about a minute had turned the fosse into a cemetery. Our heavies were now pounding the houses south-east of the fosse, and substantial-looking brick cottages were lifted bodily into the air from time to time; but it was evident by now that Loos was to be no walk-over, and in spite of a large capture of prisoners, guns, and territory, it did not look as if there was to be any piercing of the line on this occasion.

On our left the 5th Brigade had had to come back, partly because we had failed to advance on their right, and partly because their bomb supply failed at a most important moment. On our immediate right little progress had been made, but farther south terrific fighting still continued, and further efforts were made io win Fosse 8, whilst Hohenzollern Redoubt, the Quarries, and Hill 70 liad all had their bloody contests. I am told by onlookers that the advance of the Guards Division against Hill 70 in artillery formation was one of the finest spectacles that soldiers could wish to witness; but although they won the top of the hill it was swept by a terrific barrage, and with terrible gaps in tlieir ranks they were forced to step back over the ridge and dig in just on our side of the crest.

On September 27th a big attack was planned again against the dump at Fosse 8, and as the wind was in the right direction we were ordered to make another effort at Cuinchy if, after sending out patrols, we found that the gas had been effective.

Final orders were issued in a hurry and had to be wired through to companies, and as I feared there might be some mistake I decided to go up to the line, so that I could personally judge what effect our gas attack was having. The gas was loosed at 5 p. m. and was to run for twenty-five minutes. I had ordered the whole of the attacking companies into dugouts, with orders only to emerge at 5.35, when patrols were to go out. When I arrived in the trenches, therefore, only the gas experts and a few sentries could be seen, and the gas was blowing beautifully over to the enemy's trenches. It was spotted at once, and immediately the Germans put up a big barrage on our trenches, whilst in less than a minute they had lit bonfires on their parapet all the way along their line opposite us.

The scene was weird in the extreme, as dusk was coming on; and whilst the clouds of yellow gas rolled over, hundreds of fires appeared at intervals along the line. These fires, our gas experts tell us, are no use and are merely used by the enemy to give his men confidence. Be that as it may, the gas certainly seemed to lift on reaching the fires, or else the effect on the chemicals was to clarify the gas.

At 5.35 p. m. our patrols went out, and I watched one which went over from where I stood. The patrol consisted of a corporal and two privates, and they had just got through our wire when a machine gun dropped one private with five bullet wounds, and the other private took cover beside his comrade. By this time machine guns were barking in all directions and the corporal walked back to the trenches, climbed over the parapet, and came to his company commander, smacked his rifle very smartly, and reported, "Enemy machine guns active, sir." If one had not realised that this brave fellow had just come from what looked like certain death, it would have been impossible to prevent oneself roaring with laughter at his matter-of-fact voice. Yes, the machine guns were active, and, what is more, directly the patrols went out the enemy lined his parapet in large numbers and our lads opened rapid fire, with the result that many a Boche rolled back; but the wire was intact and the enemy were unaffected by the gas, and so I ordered the whole of the attackers except snipers and sentries back to their dugouts whilst the enemy barrage continued.

To revert to the patrols. The Germans began to fire on the wounded man lying out, and the earth was flying up round where he lay, so a young sergeant of the Herts ran out to him, lifted him on his back and brought him in, a very gallant act amongst the many courageous deeds of those days.

Nearly all the patrols who went out that evening were wiped out, and it was a fine thing to find men so ready to volunteer to walk in No Man's Land, and so prove whether it was possible for their comrades to advance, when most probably they would pay with their lives in the act of proof.

Once again, considering the terrific bombardment, our losses had been slight; and although we had not been over the top we believe we inflicted thirty or forty casualties, whilst ours could be counted on one l and. This was the more remarkable as tl. e two companies in support had to go up and come back a conununication trench which was heavily barraged.

On September SOtli we were relieved by the 9th Cheshh'es, and as this was the first time we had been reheved by tlie New Army we were very much interested in otir rchevers, who proved to be a fine stamp of men. The rehef only started late, and we arrived back in Betliune in the early honrs of the morning, very much fatigued after a very prolonged tour in the trenches. For months the Herts had never been out of the shell area, and when we were not in the line we were digging under fire, and this had continued for six weeks on end; and, as a matter of fact, we had had no rest for more than one week since December 1914. The longed-for holiday was not to be yet, and we soon got orders to move back to the guns, and this time we were ordered to the centre of the big battlefield. Marching to Ver-melles, which we reached at dusk, we found the village a still more battered wreck than before, as the Hun gunners had been busy with this little place all through the recent fighting. In the history of this war few spots will be more proudly remembered than Vermelles, for it was here that the French, nine months before, fought their way, yard by yard, and house to house, in a battle which lasted months.

We arrived at Vermelles just before dusk and proceeded along the Hulluch road just as it became dark. Heavy firing could be heard in front, and after we had gone a few hundred yards, bullets began to splash all round us in menacing fashion. So I decided, although the communication trench was a quagmire, that we would use it, and one by one the whole battalion dropped in to the deep trench, whilst the companies in rear lay down flat in the road. We had about a mile to go up that trench, and the going was terrible, as the trench had collapsed in many parts, the telephone wires were a network of obstacles across the track, the footboards were broken where they existed, and the mud was in its most slippery condition. To add to all our troubles our guides had not turned up, but fortunately I had been round the line in daylight, and

I hoped to fetch up right. We entered the trench at 7.30 p. m., and not till 1 o'clock was my last company in position. Had we gone on down the road we should have got to our trench by 8.30; but I had learnt in this war that the greatest thing is the preservation of British lives, and this was emphasised that night, for whereas we had two casualties, a battalion starting after us, which took this road, lost thirty-seven, although they beat us by two hours.

The line we held was a support line immediately in rear of the Quarries, that scene of violent fighting which was held by the 1st Battalion of the K. R. R., and we actually held the old British front trenches from which the attack started.

The trench was littered with equipment and all the signs of heavy work.

Away on our left the fighting at Hohen-zollern Redoubt never seemed to cease, the bursting of bombs and trench mortars continuing incessantly. Once or twice we heard sharp firing in front, and then star shells would light the scene; and on one such occasion I stood up on a fire step to see what was up, and I found myself looking into the face of a man a foot away on the parapetâ a dead man.

When dawn came we set to work to clear the battlefield, and collected hundreds of rifles, equipment, etc., and sent them all down to the collecting dump, and the companies got to work in reliefs to repair our trenches, which were much knocked about by artillery fire.

At midday I got a request from the 60th Rifles to lend them a company, as things were hot in front. Our machine guns had already gone up the previous evening.

At night we started to dig new communicating trenches forward to the 60th, so that we could reinforce under cover, and by dawn we had two quite respectable ditches up to them, along which men could march unseen.

We also sent out parties during night to bury all the dead we had marked during the day, and the battlefield soon began to look more normal.

During this day we were shelled, but as we had lots of room, we managed to move the men about directly the sheuing began, and thus avoided casualties. On the third day we heard that the Guards Division were coming in to relieve us, and our old friends, the 2nd Grenadiers, were to take over from us, and the 2nd Coldstream to reheve the 60th.

All the afternoon the 60th and our forward company were heavily shelled, and it became clear that Boche was going to counter attack. So we dispatched parties forward with bombs to our comrades in front, and up they went through the barrage with their loads.

About four o'clock the firing became very intense round the Quarries, and our front line was heavily shelled; and just as the Grenadiers came up to relieve us, the line in front became a hell of din and we were reluctant to depart whilst our No. 1 Company was " sticking it " out there.

As we marched off our guns started an intense fire, and we knew that an attack was taking place, so when we arrived at the Brigade Head-quarters dug-out, the regiment lay down whilst I went in to ask the Brigadier if we were wanted before marching off. Just at that moment a messenger arrived at the brigade office with a most urgent message for bombs and bombers, and the Brigadier asked us to help. Our men were very tired, and I went out to them as they lay resting on the side of a trench and called for volunteers to go down to Vermelles and carry up bombs. In a minute a hundred tired men, who knew they had a long march before them, were off at a double for Ver-melles, and very soon the Herts bombers and carrying parties were once again winding up the long trench with their heavy burdens.

When they arrived the 60th were at the end of their bomb supply, and very grateful they were for our reinforcement.

We then learnt that the 60th had indeed had a warm time. During that day two Herts machine guns had been buried, and in one case with all the team knocked out, save one; the sole survivor had dug his gun and ammunition out and had mounted his gun again just in time to open fire on a stream of Germans rushing up a shallow communication trench to the attack. For hours a bomb fight had been joined, but every attack of the enemy was beaten back, and eventually the Coldstream took over and the last of the Herts were on the march back to Bethune, where, thoroughly exhausted, they arrived in the early hours of the morning.

This time we really did get some rest, and the Battle of Loos, as far as the British were concerned, was over.

On October 8th we were holding a big concert in the theatre when distant firing assumed an ominous tone, and a messenger rushed into the theatre to say the 5th and 6th Brigades will return at once to billets. I sent out messengers all over Bethune, and then we got our orders to move. Within half an hour of the receipt of the order all rations were served out and water bottles full, and we paraded in the dark in the Grande Place, with only two men absent, and marched off with much singing back towards the line.

We bivouacked at Beuvry and waited for orders and news. Something was happening, and we realised that the Germans were making a big counter-attack.

We soon had our bivouac fixed, and then the men sang songs round camp fires, whilst the other battahons of the brigade came marching up in the dark to the rendezvous.

Cookers were ordered up, and a hot meal was just finished, and we were ready for anything when news came through that the enemy had made a great effort to regain his lost ground, but that all his efforts had withered up in front of the British line, and that he had bumped especially into the Guards Division with great disaster. The Guards had had a good shoot, and so had the neighbouring divisions, and the official news next day was to the effect that the German attack had failed completely, with a loss of 8,000 casualties. This was the last and greatest effort of the Germans to win back the victory of Loos. This offensive had proved that, given sufficient munitions, the German line can be stormed, but that the limited objective is at present the wise course and that the problem of strong posts is still unsolved, unless each objective can be hammered in turn. Loos, with all its losses, has however given us a feeling of moral superiority over the Boche, and perhaps the Loos salient mav some dav be of 164 FAREWELL TO THE HERTS pt. i value when we cross the Vimy Ridge to the south.

Now began a tedious winter, with many tours in the trenches between Loos and Festubert, in which we had to sit still under many bombardments and, as Christmas approached, had to contend with much water, so much so that at Festubert we had to content oui elvcs with holding islands; and all the breastworks we had built with such great care gradually collapsed under our eyes, and all we could do was to repeatedly rebuild our islands.

Two battalions of the New Army came into our brigade and two of the old regular battalions departed. One of the new battalions was attached to us for instruction, the

13th Essex, and great friends we became. Months afterwards this battalion greatly distinguished itself on the Somme.

Another time the Footballci-s' Battalion of the Royal Fusiliers sent companies to us in the trenches for instruction, and I remember one company came up into the line just as a very heavy shelling was taking placeâ a trying moment for new hands.

I was leading the company into the front line when I suddenly heard one of the Footballers blow a shrill blast on his whistle. I turned round and asked what the devil he was doing, and he replied, "Well, sir, I thought it was just about 'arf time."

Christmas comes, and this time we have a great officers' banquet at the La France Hotel, and much feasting amongst all ranks, football, drill, and high spirits. The winter drags out its weary course and the army is gradually growing in numbers and guns, and next time we shall see.

On February 6th I received orders to take command of a Brigade.

I was naturally pleased at promotion, but it is with a heavy heart that you leave men with whom you have lived in the palace of death for sixteen months, and my feelings were the more sad because my lads had shown those qualities of loyalty and devotion to duty which makes one feel that they are friends who make campaigning a joy.

The "Herts Guards" won great favour in all the area of the Bethune district, and wherever we went the inhabitants would turn out to show how glad they were to see 166 FAREWELL TO THE HERTS pt. i us again, and never once did I have a serious complaint of their conduct from civilians. Crime was practically non-existent and sickness slight.

A curious fact with regard to sickness was, that whenever we were due for the trenches, no one reported sick, and apparently it was considered in the ranks bad form to go sick if there was any danger about. These are the little things which make one so proud of the British soldiers in France, for it proves that in spite of " grousing," " swearing," and other little vices, there is nobility there, which proves that, given the chance, our race still possesses all that goes to make men great.

So on a February morning I said goodbye to the Herts, and saw them march by for the last time. I conjured up recollections of the days when these fine men, as boys, used to march up to the park at home for little field days; how we went together to tlie range and to camp; and how the old volunteers became the Territorials. I had seen them grow up, and for yeai's we had played at soldiers together, and then, when the great adventure called, the Herts had responded, andâ God bless them!â they have been through a thousand hells and have

CH. xxxi "THE HERTS GUARDS" 167 ever remained soldiers and gentlemen. They had not been found wanting,

Note, â The Herts, months after I left them, were in the attack at Thiepval, at Swaben, and in the big attack in the Ancre, where, advancing for 1,600 yards in perfect order, they captured their objective in masterly form, took some 300 prisoners, cohBolidated and repelled counter-attacks, and marched back with a minimum number of casualties.

Again, in July 1917, the Herts advanced in magnificent style, but on reaching their objective found themselves "in the air," with unbroken wire in front of them. Thev were attacked on three sides and a desperate fight ensued. Every single officer was either killed or wounded, but the Herts fought on first under the sergeant-major, then when he fell under a sergeant, and finally the remnants retired fighting doggedly under the chaplain, and dug in. In this action Colonel Page, the gallant commander, was killed whilst organising a counter-attack.

On February 8th, 1916, I sped northwards in a motor and came to Erquinghem, near Armentieres, to take over the command of the Infantry Brigade on the very night that the brigade was going up to the trenches. Armentieres, which is just behind the British Hne, was interesting to me, as one of my forbears was governor of that city some centuries before the entente cordiale. It is with an odd feehng that one enters new surroundings in a new country and finds oneself amongst strangers, and I must confess to the sensation of a new boy at school when I arrived at my headquarters.

My embarrassment was not lessened when I found that all my battalion commanders were men of previous war experience and very much my senior in age, but I soon found that they were determined to make my task easy; and in spite of the fact that

I was a Territorial and they all regulars, I realised that I was dealing with men to whom the war came first, with personal considerations buried a long way behind.

When the history of the New Army comes to be written, no mean tribute should be paid to the ex-regulars who, in many cases, had to build up and instruct the new units practically single-handed, as frequently they had no one of any previous military knowledge to assist them. On those menâ who had in some cases left active life behind, and who again got into harness and, after most exacting preparation, led their battalions to France with all the discomforts of trench life, all the nerve-racking din of modern war and all the responsibility of leading raw troopsâ the strain must have been great, and all honour is due to these fine English gentlemen for the great part they played.

The Brigade Infantry consisted of four battalions of the New Army, two battalions of the Northumberland Fusiliers and two of the Durham Light Infantry. No battalion had more than two officers with previous military service, and none were on the active list at the outbreak of war.

The non-commissioned officers were equally inexperienced, very few having seen any kind of military service prior to the war.

The men were fine, big fellows, many of whom were miners, a likely lot to do credit to the bayonet when opportunity offered. â

My head-quarters were in a farm which was also occupied by its owners, for here the cultivation of the soil went on well forward of Brigade Head-quarters.

To reach the line we usually rode to a shattered village which was frequently shelled, and went thence by communication trenches to the front system, which at this time of the year was in a poor state owing to the weather. Only breastworks were possible, owing to the watery state of the soil and the fact that we were on a level with the river Lys and its several small tributaries which run by and through the trenches. The result of this watery ground was, that great sections of breastwork were continually falling in, and the troops led a very muddy and uninteresting existence, with occasional patrol encounters in No Man's Land, which was wider in these parts than I had yet experienced. When after about fifteen days we had orders to the effect that the division was to be reheved, I was not sorry, for six months in this part of the world, with no chance of training, was hardly conducive to improvement, and all ranks were " fed np " with this dull flat land.

We guessed we should go south, and we guessed right; but first we marched to the Kazebrucke neighbourhood, which I had not visited since November 1914, and we marched thither on a very frosty morning along very slippery roads.

We discovered that our mobility was not quite perfect, and winged words flew around; but we knew that our stationary life was chiefly responsible, and we determined to improve.

After a day or two's rest, the brigade entrained for Bruay area, and was billeted in Marles-les-Mines and district. Here we spent a few days getting fit and drilling, and our miners made friendly invasions against the French mines, and many of our men were not satisfied until they had had a shift in the pits. We now heard that our division was to be attached to another corps, and we moved up to billets in Fresni-court district.

This country of Artois is a jolly change after Flanders, as there are hills and woods and comfortable quarters, with many commodious chateaux and capital huts for the men.

The division was now ordered to take over from the French the hne in front of Souchez village, with one brigade in the line, one in support, and our own in reserve.

This was to me by far the most fascinating spot I had yet visited, and I spent many hours examining the immortal battlefield where France won back the great spur of Notre Dame de Lorette and fought and won her bloody hand-to-hand fights in Souchez and Carency, with the culminating blow which secured the slopes of Vimy Ridge and almost won the ridge itself.

No soldiers could want a more interesting ramble than round this historic field, the only drawback being that Vimy Ridge frowns down on you from its great brown mass, and if you linger too long on the road Boche snipes at you with field guns, which is an attention far too personal to be appreciated.

As you approach Ablain St. Nazaire village, Notre Dame leaves its sloping green surface and becomes more precipitous and rocky, great ravines run into the southern face, from which ideal artillery positions French guns were noisily and with many an echo rolling up the hill pouring their wrath upon the enemy. Here the guns were ensconced behind an almost sheer wall of hillside, and nothing apparently except an enemy howitzer could stop them at their business. Ablain village is a scarred and battered place, and there the underground life is the mode, for if any group of men or any vehicle honoured the street, then a bouquet of shrapnel would send you running for dear life. So the transport only creeps up after dark, and the individual by day is not wont to Jinger.

Here I entered what I believed was my future head-quartersâ a week afterwards it was vacated as dangerousâ and then I passed on down the village and saw the remains of the church, just one face of the tower still standing silhouetted against Notre Dame, which made an imposing background; and there one sees the great strength of the spur itself rising almost sheer up out of Souchez valley, and we could almost picture the blue Poilu as he hunted the grey Boche down the side of that cuff.

We then come to the sugar factory, levelled to the ground by months of shelling, a piece of twisted machinery surrounded by bricks marking the place where the sucrerie had been, around which hundreds died in some of the fiercest fighting of the war. Close by is the cemetery, where the hallowed ground was churned up to such an extent that the dead, ancient and modern, lay side by side, and perhaps the spirits of the heroes of Conde's great fights stretched a hand to France's newest dead and hailed them worthy of the soil.

Carency, once a village, now only a glorious name, lies beside the Souchez river, where the guns of France had to blast their way and where, ever since, the German gunners had spat out their wrath.

Prior to Verdun, with the possible exception of Ypres, no country had claimed such a toll of dead as this, and even when we arrived there were many signs of this year-old death grip.

On the top of Notre Dame there lay a German, and prone across him a Frenchman. Each had given and each received the coup de grace. Surely the withered remains.

which still lay there on the crest of the hill at the time I speak of, were a symbol of that great conflict, and perhaps a little more; for although both died, the Frenchman was on topâ and then the British came.

The snow had cleared away and the weather began to improve when we heard of a change of plan and moved north of the Notre Dame Ridge, with orders for the division to take over the three-brigade front from the Souchez river to the railway north of Calonne.

To the Brigade was allotted the

Calonne sector, where we relieved old comrades of mine.

Calonne itself is a mining village which is situated right on the line of trenches, the eastern face of the village actually forming part of the front line, whilst, almost opposite Calonne, is the Cite de Corneillcs on the German front system. This was a most interesting sector and very strongly fortified. One feature of the front trench was peculiar, because the line ran over a big slag heap which was always on lire, and had been so for, I believe, some fifty years, and whenever the enemy shelled the heap it was inclined to burst into flames. The trench was not pleasant in Calonne village, because, when the enemy shelled, many bricks flew around, and if a piece of shell missed you, you always had a chance of a brickbat.

The line, which had recently been taken over from the French, required a good deal of work, but the communication trenches in Calonne were remarkably well built and revetted with pit props.

From Calonne back to Bully Grenay, there was no covered way, and the road was overlooked by the enemy, which made it very unpleasant by day when it was shelled, and more so by night as bullets were numerous; so much so, that we had a few casualties on the way up to relieve on the first night.

So I made up my mind to spend the first part of our time in making our defences strong and providing a good communication trench, and the whole brigade put its back into the work of improving the line.

After a short time we got the front line perfect and the support line fair; and, simultaneously, the two resting battalions dug two magnificent communication trenches.

My head-quarters at the start were in

Calonne village, but as two enemy high explosives penetrated the upper storey one night whilst I was at dinner, my Divisional General told me to establish new quarters at Bully Grenay, where we were most comfortable, in spite of occasional shelling.

Calonne had now become so strong and its communications so good, that I decided to encourage offensive tactics, and this seemed the more desirable as our comrades on our right had very poor trenches, whereas we had good shelters and cellars, and it was therefore expedient from every point of view to draw fire and waste enemy ammunition, especially as our position was so strong that we rather invited hostilities in any form.

Night after night, therefore, we sallied forth with small fighting patrols in No Man's Land, which succeeded in running into several Boehe working parties and inflicting many casualties, whilst all day our snipers kept adding to our bag.

I was very proud of my sector, and we had numerous visitors. One day, the Corps Commander, Sir Henry Wilson, desired to see our reserve line, so I conducted him down our new-made communication trench, when, to my annoyance, the enemy began shelling the trench, just by what is known as Conde's tree, near a monument to the same celebrity. I accordingly, thinking myself very wise, suggested to my distinguished visitor that we should take a circuitous route round some old trenches. As bad luck would have it, the German shells pursued us away to the flank. At last, feeling rather hot, we arrived in the reserve line, and here I thought by doubling to the right again we should surely avoid our persecutors. Not a bit of it; German shrapnel kept on bursting within twenty yards of us, or less, and I bethought me of a gunners' observation post where there was a shallow dugout, and down the steps of this haven we jumped, only to get a couple of direct hits on the dugout itself. In a minute or two we decided to push on, and only reached peaceful surroundings when we got to Calonne village. Here I assured the Corps Commander everything would be quiet, and I was just describing the virtues of the village line when the enemy again commenced firing, and so we again beat a retreat towards home. What the Corps Commander thought of his " happy Sunday afternoon " with me I do not know, but as he cracked jokes the whole time, I hope he enjoyed it.

A day or two afterwards, Sir Hubert Gough, the Corps Commander immediately on my left, desired a guide to see where we joined up, and I sallied forth with him and a goodly company of Staff officers. We came to the railway on the left of the Calonne sector, and the general expressed a desire to see a machine gun emplacement which swept the railway towards the enemy. I expostulated, as it was a very bright day, but a Staff officer of the next division thought it was safe, so down the railway the general and a Staff officer went, and I folloaved a hundred yards behind, so as not to form too noticeable a group, and the remainder of the party waited for us to return. The Huns saw us and opened fire with field guns just as the Corps Commander reached the machine gun dugout, and in he tumbled; but I was not so lucky, as I had no holeâ only the bare bank of the embankment, on which I spreadcagled whilst half a dozen shrapnel burst along the railway, missing me by a very few yards.

I remained in my uncomfortable position until the famous general came running back, doing a half-mile in good time, and then I followed, with a record sprint.

My Cook's Tours with Corps Com- manders were getting rather too warm to be amusing.

Now I was anxious to kill Boches opposite Calonne, and the corps was anxious to strafe the famous Pimple on Vimy Ridge; and as it was undesirable that the enemy should ' counter strafe" our poor trenches at Souchez, the two schemes appeared to offer good co-operative results. My plan was to make the enemy think we were going to attack him and get him to man his trenches and bring up supports, and then give him a really heavy bombardment whilst we were safely stowed away in dugouts and cellars. To excite the enemy and to add to the illusion, we dug assembly trenches two days before, and made considerable preparations, cutting wire with artillery, and by night raking the gaps with machine guns; and on the morning of April 10th we made a great display of scaling ladders in the reserve line, and half a dozen heroes, with fixed bayonets, kept on marching round this line and successfully drew fire.

At 1.30 we began to bombard the enemy, and showed more bayonets in the reserve line. Our bombardment was quite considerable, and whilst our field howitzers were playing havoc with the houses in the Cite de Corneilles, a 9-inch howitzer pumped sixty rounds at a great pit head which overlooked our line, causing great delight to all beholders. At about four o'clock we gave an intense bombardment of all guns, mortars, and about 200 rifle grenades, and then suddenly we let loose sham gas, which blew over to the enemy's trenches, and all guns lifted. Now we could hear the Germans shouting " Gaz " and beating gongs for dear life, and at a given signal, all our guns came down again on the German trenches, and all our mortars and rifle grenadiers opened a few rounds and then took cover.

There is no doubt that we thoroughly deceived the enemy, who must have been thick in his trenches when our guns shortened and all our missiles hurtled at him whilst the smoke blew over, and as a result, he put up a very big barrage between our front and support trenches where none of our men were, and where none intended to go, because we were all, like " brer Fox," lying very low and thoroughly enjoying the noise.

The enemy was seen to line his parapet, and our snipers had the time of their lives, and at a conservative estimate we are sure that wc inflicted in these operations thirty visible casualties, apart from what our guns may have done. Our total casualties were one officer and six other ranks, and the enemy wasted nearly 2,000 rounds of shell on us whilst we were under cover. The result of this operation was, that all ranks, both infantry and gunners, felt that we had thoroughly punished the enemy.

After these episodes the " stuff " began to fly a bit, and Calonne lost some of its houses, but we kept up our offensive tactics, and the Durhams on the left got home one night with grcfl, t effect by a bomb attack on a working party, whilst the Northumber-lands on the right also created a diversion which unhappily did not come off.

Here there were two saps, very close together, being only about twenty yards apart, with very thick wire in between; and as our sap was in hand-bombing distance of the enemy, we decided to make an effort to destroy the enemy's sap. In order to do this and clear away the huge mass of wire entanglement, we determined to try and blow the wire up with an explosive torpedo. We secured a torpedo, and two very gallant men from the Northumberland Fusiliers crawled out at night with the six-foot torpedo and succeeded in placing it under the German wire and lighting the fuse, when they hurriedly retired. Unhappily, however, something was amiss with the torpedo, and it did not go off, and the same men crawled out again and brought the torpedo back, very angry at having run such risks for nothing.

At this same spot a most unfortunate incident occurred. The Adjutant of the Northumberland Fusiliers, Captain the Hon. J. G. Joicey, an extremely gallant officer, went out to examine the wire, and was unfortunately killed by a bomb between the two saps. Several efforts were made the same night, under heavy fire, to recover his body, and a gallant volunteer actually crawled out and tied a wire round the body; but when our men in the sap began to pull on the wire, it unhappily snapped.

Now we were afraid that possibly Captain Joicey had maps or information on him when killed, and so we decided the next night to make a big effort to try and bring him in, and our plan was to open intense artillery and mortar fire on the German sap and then to rush out and bring him in. Unhappily, the enemy conceived the same idea, and a quarter of an hour before our bombardment was to commence, they opened a terrific fire and secm'ed the body in the confusion.

After about a fortnight we were reueued in the Calonne sector by another brigade, and went back to rest.

After leaving the Calonne sector the brigade went out to the rest area, where for the first time since it arrived in France we were able to undergo serious training. We were quartered in various villages near the river Lys, and practised open warfare, and a very marked improvement in discipline, drill, marching, and field work was soon evident.

After a happy and strenuous time we marched back by easy stages to the Bruay district, and from thence, after a few days as brigade in reserve, we went into the line immediately north of the Souchez river and relieved the 24th Brigade.

This sector was in very poor condition, the front trenches being constantly blown in by trench mortar and shell fire on the left, whilst the right was absolutely dominated by the enemy on Vimy Ridge, which looked straight down on our system. The enemy snipers were very active here, and a few men got shot in the head the first forty-eight hours in, so I determined to deepen the whole of the right and to make a complete new support line and communication trenches. We had a prolonged stay in this line, and the conditions got more lively as the time went on; but thanks to the good weather and hard work, before we handed over to our successors we had a fair front line, a perfect support line, and a good reserve line in the front system.

The trench was on the lower slope of the spur, and here, as in the front system, digging was difficult owing to the large number of graves of French and German deadâ killed in the great fighting of a year before.

I mentioned in a previous chapter that the trenches on the Vimy slopes south of the Souchez river were very poor, and this fact the enemy who dominated them also apparently realised, for after a terrific bombardment he made a big attack on the division on our right and their neighbours. The London Territorials' trenches were almost completely destroyed, and when the German avalanche rushed down the hill upon them, their front line did not give, but died gamely, and so the gallant little

Cockneys were overwhelmed and the Germans advanced farther down the slopes of Vimy.

I watched this attack with considerable anxiety from Notre Dame. The din was hideous, and I could see the star shells ever coming closer on my right. It transpired that the Germans had advanced 800 to 1,000 yards, and if they had come another 1,000 yards we should have been involved, but the attack was now held.

A night attack on Vimy, viewed from Notre Dame, was a wonderful spectacle. The firework display, looking up on the height, was wonderful, as lights and rockets went up in scores, and the flashes of thousands of bursting shells added to the extraordinary effect, whilst the echo of the guns and shell bursts along the Souchez valley were weird in the extreme.

About this time I organised a raid for June 2nd, which was duly carried out by the Durham Light Infantry. I favoured a small raid, and twenty-five picked officers and men were told off for the work. Twice during the day the group of artillery covering us gave an intense bombardment.

whilst our mortars cut a gap in the wire, and the idea was, for the infantry to leave our trenches whilst our field artillery was actually firing on the enemy trench and whilst our mortars were firing over the heads of the infantry.

When I state that the trenches at the point selected were just under seventy yards apart, it will be realised that we had some confidence in our artillery.

Punctual to the moment, as our artillery commenced one minute's intense bombardment, the raiders left our trench and were crossing our wire whilst our shells were bursting on the German trench. Precisely at the minute's conclusion, the guns on the objective ceased, and those to either flank continued. Our raiders entered the German trench without casualty, and separated according to plan. Breathless moments these for the raiding party. The officer leading ran straight into two Huns and shot them both; they continued along the pitch-dark trench when they came to a sap. The second officer, turning down here, suddenly sees a German; he snaps at him with an automatic pistol which misfires, the German fires his rifle and misses at two yards and charges with his bayonet; again the automatic pistol fails to fire, when, by the greatest luck, the first officer, hearing the noise, rushes up and there, in the narrow sap, shoots the German dead over the shoulder of his friend.

A Durham in the main trench is now engaged in a life-and-death bayonet fight with a huge German. The officer dare not fire his revolver, because parry and thrust, advance and retreat go on between these two, and to shoot might be fatal to the wrong man; but the Durham lad was no chicken, and after as pretty a bout as can be desired, he killed his man.

Meanwhile, a sergeant, leading the party which turns right, bayonets three Germans in quick succession, and the bombing party is at work. Five great dugouts, lit by electricity and teeming with Germans, are duly bombed, and death is dealt with a free hand.

I had given implicit orders that I must have a live German for identification purposes, and a small Durham was accordingly marching off a huge Hun when suddenly, in the pitch-dark, the German realises he is near the entrance to a dugout which was unknown to our man, so he hurls himself down the dugout entrance, lugging the escort with him. Just as the Durham is disappearing down the hole, one of his comrades arrives on the scene and, by slinging his bayonet down the hole, kills the big man just in time, and so perishes my live Hun.

Now the whistle blows and the raiders retire through the gap in the wire, which had been cut by a special party detailed, and a rocket goes up, and guns, mortars, and grenades all pour in their fire to cover the retirement of the raiders, whilst Lewis and machine guns rake the enemy trench right and left, and behold, the whole of the raiders are back safe, and one may be excused a sigh of relief. In this raid, where fighting in the trench was carried on hand to hand, the Durhams slew, with bayonet and bullet, twelve Germans; and at the lowest estimate, killed twelve Germans in each of the five dugouts bombed, or seventy-two Germans killed.

Our total casualties were two men very slightly wounded by the back splash of their own bombs.

The whole operation took three minutes; a fairly intense three minutes this, and fine work; but we knew that we owed much to the perfect shooting of the guns and mortars, for a single error of a few yards by a gun might have spoilt the whole show.

Our raid enraged the Boche, and life be- came unhealthy in these parts from now onwards. My head-quarters were in a little farmhouse, and the village came in for a tremendous shelling, and we had some lively times.

One day, while we w ere sitting in our mess room with the signalling officer at the table, a terrific crash occurred, and a time-fuse whistled past my leg, which it obligingly missed by inches, and we discovered that the two adjoining bedrooms, happily unoccupied, as the brigade-major and orderly officer were out, were demolished by a 5 9 high explosive.

This kind of thing makes one rather nippy, and next day, when a high explosive burst in the farmyard twenty yards away, I " got the wind up " and yelled " to dugouts." We all cleared, and had just got round the wall of the house when the next shell demolished the mess room where we had all been sitting fifteen seconds beforeâ which only proves that it is well to be active in such times.

Meanwhile, our village was becoming more and more dusty and noisy; houses were knocked down right and left, and the last of the inhabitants were prevailed upon to leave.

One night a party of marines from the Naval Brigade were marching up to dig, and as I watched them go by, a shell pitched in the midst of one group and three were killed and two wounded.

The enemy bombardment against our trenches was particularly violent, and the point from which we raided was daily destroyed by mortars.

A newly arrived division now sent up companies for instruction, and I was rather amused, going round the line at night, to hear very disparaging remarks concerning our trenches as compared to those at Galli-poli. " This, sir, is child's play," I was told, " compared to that."

The next night, after their trenches had been half levelled, I asked them how the child's play was getting on, and they frankly confessed a desire for the quiet life of Suvla Bay.

We were determined not to be cowed by the enemy's frightfulness, and gave them three mortars for every one they fired at us, and by very gallant work on the part of our mortar teams we almost silenced the enemy's mortars after a few days.

We also decided to raid one of his saps on the right, and twelve men of the Northumberland Fusiliers, under an officer, on June 8th, discovering that the sap was heavily held, made a converging attack from two flanks. When within about twelve yards of the sap, unhappily one of the attackers fell over the trip wire on a steel plate, whereupon the enemy opened fire. The attacking party, therefore, heavily bombed the sap and retired according to orders. As the sap was at the time crowded with Germans, we had good reason to believe that many casualties were inflicted by our bombers, whilst ours were nil.

The division was now relieved, and another division took over our sector whilst we marched back by easy stages to the training area. Our first stop was in a very charming little village where British troops had not previously been billeted. I was riding on to the chateau with my Staff, a little ahead of the brigade, when I noticed a great deal of excitement amongst the inhabitants, who were running in all directions, with turkeys, geese, and fowls of lesser dignity under their arms. When I inquired from my officer interpreter, a gallant Frenchman, the reason for this agitation, he informed me that the inhabitants were convinced that we would clear the place of every kind of animal, and that therefore all the live stock was being conveyed to cellars, etc. I had my little joke at their expense, and desired him to convey to the citizens that British soldiers were not living on the country, and that I guaranteed the lives of their birds, whereupon, with much cackling, our feathered friends were allowed to resume their normal existence and the inhabitants proceeded to offer them for sale at outrageous prices, and that night we ate an enormous goose in our messâ the goose was paid for.

The chateau in which I was billeted was an old house, the property of a French marquise whose ancestors looked down upon us from the walls as we dined. I cannot help thinking that these said ancestors were almost as confus' 'd as the inhabitants, especially so when I discovered that our horses were tied up to the identical iron rings which were placed there by British cavalry 100 years ago in the days when the British and French were not allies.

We again found ourselves in the training area, where wc had progressive training, ending up in divisional field days, and all ranks of the division greatly improved, when the usual joke went round that we were being "fed up for slaughter"; and then came the great day when we were entrained for the Somme, towards the end of July.

CH. v THE BOMBARDMENT BEGINS 201

We detrained at Amiens, where all was bustle, and the crowded city was much interested at our arrival. Amiens was like nothing we had yet seen in Franceâ civil life continued, all the shops were doing a roaring trade, and all sorts of vegetables and fruit found its way into our various messes.

My head-quarters were established in a delightful little chateau within 300 yards of the Somme, and here we watched troop trains coming up at intervals of every five minutes. And now the great bombardment for the July offensive commenced, and the distant sky at night was lit by a thousand flashes.

Brigadiers were ordered to go up and reconnoitre all the approaches to the British lines, and we spent a very instructive day, motoring all along immediately behind our line and watching the tremendous bombardment of the British guns. Our artillery superiority and our ascendancy in the air were very noticeable, and at the commencement the duel appeared to be very one-sided.

The nature of the country, with its rolling downs, lent itself very well to observation, and after a very noisy but intensely interest- ing day we motored back to our commands; and now, each day, we marched forward by easy stages and bivouacked at Millencourt, just in rear of Albert, when the great attack commenced.

On July 3rd the brigade moved up to Albert, where we lay in trenches for one night. The weather, which was happily fine at the commencement of the operations, continued to be so, and we did not suffer any discomfort from our night out.

The whole of the organisation behind the lines was most interesting, and showed a marked improvement on anything we had yet experienced; and indeed all things looked like business.

In folds of the ground west of Albert there were long lines of guns and howitzers of such calibre that if any one of them had arrived in France in 1914 the whole Army would have wanted to visit so unusual a monster and been overjoyed at its arrival, and as we marched by this formidable line and saw each gun or howitzer jump and make its bow to the enemy, and the teams 204 THE BATTLE OF THE SOMME pt. ii sweating as they hauled fresh shells into position, we felt much exhilarated.

From Albert we marched on July 4th to Becourtwood, where the brigade bivouacked. Here the din was so incessant that it was impossible to sleep, and by way of adding to our discomfort rain began to fall and the wood was shelled by enemy field guns.

By this time, of course, tlie British Army had captured the whole of the first system of trenches on our front, and our division came up in time for the second series of operations, and was allocated the objective, Contalmaison village, to a point just west of Bailiff Wood, both inclusive, and I was informed that one brigade would be responsible for the objective from the western point of Contalmaison village across the valley running thence to Bailiff Wood, the wood itself, and thence to Point 81 on the high groimd crossing the western slope of the valley.

Before we could attack this ultimate objective the division would have to capture some intermediate trenches, and I sallied forth with my brigade-major to reconnoitre as far as the enemy permitted.

We were glad to get away from the everlasting din of Becourt Wood and made our way towards the original British line. Here we saw the first signs of the great battle, as dead horses lay in pathetic attitudes where a battery had been rushed up to support the attack. Passing on, we crossed the old . fortified Germem Trenches â Genman Conrimunication Trenches â Â I â I t Li ht RejIwa

PLAN SHOWING THE JOINT ATTACKS BY THE BRIGADE ON THE SOMMB.

British line and walked over what had been No Man's Land, that wonderful continuous racecourse where a hundred thousand British soldiers had charged with light heart through a rain of lead only three days before.

206 THE BATTLE OF THE SOMME pt. n

Here losses had not been very heavy, and just where we passed not many British dead were visible, but burial parties were out, and soon the battlefield would show little sign of that wonderful rush which heralded the great July. We now reached the old German first line and saw the extraordinary havoc our guns had wrought. The wire was smashed and buried in a thousand craters, and the trench itself was for every few yards obliterated or choked with earth.

As German shells were now falling with some persistence we decided to use what cover the old German trenches afforded, and we saw many a ghastly spectacle: occasional khaki figures lay prone in the trench, and then perhaps a group of dead in grey almost blocking our passage. Sometimes we got out of the trench to avoid these sights, but safety demanded our return to cover, and we were very much relieved when we found ourselves on a sunk road by Lozenge Wood, which was being heavily shelled at that moment, so we edged off westward, and there got a distant view of Contalmaison village and the tops of the trees at Bailiff Wood, returning again over the stricken field to Becourt.

On July 5th we got the splendid news that a brigade of our division, at a second attempt, had captured Horseshoe Trench, and received our orders to attack the main objective on July 7th as part of a big attack by large forces on each of our flanks. We therefore relieved the brigade in Horseshoe Trench, and I gave orders to the leading battalion to capture and consolidate a trench known as the Triangle that night. This operation was successfully carried out by the D. L. I, after dark without opposition. The big attack was due to start at 8 a. m. on July 7th, but as a brigade of our division had the difficult task of capturing the whole length of the village, I got instructions that I was to wait until they were level with me before starting. As therefore the heavy artillery was ordered to fire on Bailiff Wood until 9.30 a. m. I gave orders 208 ATTACK ON BAILIFF WOOD pt. ii to the attacking battalion, the Northumberland Fusiliers, not to assault until 9.15 a. m.

I heard that the next brigade were well under way and had reached the southernmost house of Contalmaison, so at 9.15 the Fusiliers went over the top.

The Germans had turned their barrage on to the valley, and it was by now a cauldron of bursting explosions.

Notwithstanding these conditions the battalion advanced with perfect order, marching in quick step right through the barrage, where things looked about as ugly as possible. On they pressed until they reached a point only fifty yards south of Bailiff Wood; but here our attacking waves came under a terrible enfilade machine gun fire from the trench running along the west of Contalmaison and also a frontal fire from Bailiff Wood and beyond. As our line of advance was entirely dominated from both flanks there was no question of digging in in the valley, as the men were being shot as they lay in the open, so I decided not to throw fresh troops in, and the centre of the Northumberland Fusiliers withdrew after three companies had made a fine effort.

A platoon of the Fusiliers, working on the right, had captured a small German work, disposing of its garrison and taking twenty-seven unwounded prisoners, and this trench we continued to hold. Another platoon, working on the left, succeeded in digging in under fire on the high ground, and were able to consolidate, thus greatly assisting later operations.

The D. L. I., according to orders, had moved up to the assembly trenches as the N. F. went over, with a view to supporting the attack; and I now sent a message to the commanding officer of this unit to try and work along the high ground to the left and gain ground towards the objective. About the same time I heard that there was a gap of 500 yards between us and the division who had advanced successfully. But this big gap left both divisions in the air. I therefore ordered the D. L. I. to fill the gap and secure the high ground in alignment with the captured line of the Division and capture the dominating enemy position on the left of our objective at Point 81. This operation was successful, a few wounded prisoners being taken.

As dusk came on I ordered the Fusiliers to push out posts in the direction of Point 81 210 ATTACK ON BAILIFF WOOD pt. ii and to endeavour to join up with the D. L. I. I also ordered a platoon to be sent to advance along the trench running north along the western face of Contal-maison, and to endeavour to establish itself there at the right of my intended objective by means of a bomb attack. This platoon came under machine gun fire, but succeeded in occupying and consolidating a German work on the railway, where they took a few wounded prisoners.

The D. L. I., after dark, assaulted and took the German redoubt at Point 81, and consolidated, sending back three wounded prisoners. This was very encouraging, as hitherto a machine gun at that point had been a most powerful obstacle to our advance.

My position was now much improved, as we held the high ground on the left of our objective, the redoubt within the left of the objective, and two works well forward in the valley, and we were therefore more or less protected by a continuous line.

Posts were pushed out along the German trench running north to Hill 81, but consolidation was rendered very difficult owing to a heavy rain, which turned the earth into a sticky bog.

It was now reported that our booty in the valley included several hundred rounds of German shell, which was safely protected by one of our advanced posts already referred to.

On July 8th consolidation went forward. At 1.30 p. m. I was ordered to occupy Bailiff Wood. I ordered the D. L. I., who had relieved the N. F. during the night, to send out strong fighting patrols, but not to involve the whole battalion without further orders.

These patrols found the wood occupied on its southern face and came under heavy machine gun fire, both from the wood, Con-talmaison, and Quadrangle Trench running along the western end of Contalmaison, and the patrols came in, having suitercd souic casualties.

During the night the D. L. I, did a fine piece of consohdation, joining up Triangle Trench and Point 81, so that I had a continuous line for the first time from where we joined the Division on our left, thence bending back to our front jumping-off trench.

The N. F. battalion, in support, had had a most trying time, carrying bombs, evacuating wounded, and consolidating in the wet under a very heavy and continuous shell fire, and had suffered many casualties without having any sort of a show.

I now decided to try and capture the rest of my objective, and this I determined to attempt from the high ground of Point 81. I ordered thedurliam battalion, at that time resting in Becourt Wood, to make this flank attack with two companies by a bombing attack along the trench running east from Point 81 to Contalmaison, the rear company to hold and consolidate the trench and facing north, as the attack progressed, and also to consolidate the eastern face of Bailiff Wood. I further ordered one battalion to endeavour to occupy the south end of Bailiff Wood during the afternoon with a strong patrol, so as to assist the attack of the D. L. I, after dusk. This patrol went out under an officer and actually entered Bailiff Wood, and only withdrew owing to the fact that our own heavies apparently had not got information of our movements and shelled the wood so heavily that it became untenable.

The artillery plan for the night attack was as follows: To bombard the trench from Point 81 eastward to Contalmaison, and at the hour of assault to Uft these guns on to the German trenches north-west of Con-talmaison, and to continue from the hour of attack an intense enfilade fire along Quadrangle Trench from Point 74 to Point 26 until 6.15 p. m.

I watched the two companies go up to the assembly trenches from my head-quarters in the old British line, and they were in fine form and full of confidence. But the best-laid plans in war are wont to be upset; there was some delay, owing to a false alarm of a German attack on our left.

In the meanwhile, my wire to our artillery group was cut, and the barrage was fired as ordered and ceased as ordered; the result was, that the D. L. I, attacked at about 8 p. m. instead of 6 p. m., and without the advantage of artillery co-operation. The Durhams proceeded with their attack and advanced east, capturing Baihff Wood, where a platoon was detached to consolidate the eastern face, and the attack succeeded in reaching a point within fifty yards of the north-west point of Contalmaison Village, where it came under a heavy machine gun fire at close range, and a strong party was seen deploying in front.

Thinking that the brigade on the right

CH. viii THE OBJECTIVE GAINED 215 might have advanced in the dark, the officer commanding the attack challenged, and heard a reply in Enghsh, "It is only us "; but recognising German uniforms, he decided to attack, and rushed forward with his leading bombers, when a machine gun at Point 25 opened fire, point blank at the attackers. The Germans now counter attacked in force over the open, and as our bomb attack was strung out, it had to give way and retired, bombing all the way back to Point 13. Here the Durhams managed to extend, and opened rapid fire on the enemy; and after detaching two strong parties north to protect their flanks, returned to the attack and drove the enemy back to the point they had originally reached when the German machine gun barred further progress.

This Point we managed to block, and the whole captured trench was consohdated with the exception of the forty yards on our extreme right which was dominated by the machine gun.

Meanwhile, the flank parties advancing north from Point 13 managed to capture four guns which had been abandoned by their teams, and proceeded to dig in in front of the guns.

This adventurous little force of about a platoon was right over the crest looking down on Pozieres village, and they were heavily counter attacked next day; but twice they drove off the attackers, who also came under our machine gun fire from the north of Bailiff Wood, and the guns were safely handed over to another brigade when the Durhams were relieved the following night.

We were now in a very much stronger position, and had won practically the whole of our objective as well as the 500 yards to our left; and when it is remembered that at the commencement of these operations the brigade was absolutely in the air on both flanks, and that our left was now secure and our right well covered from Baihff Wood and the high ground to the west, we were naturally feeling not altogether dissatisfied.

In spite of three most gallant frontal attacks by the brigade on our right, who had twice entered the village, Contalmaison still remained German. It was therefore decided that another brigade, which was the least exhausted in the division, should attack it from the ground we had captured, advancing east in the same way as we had attacked Bailiff Wood. The advantage of this method lay in the fact that troops could reach their assembly position without being observed and they had only 700 yards to go across the open; also the enemy would not be so likely to expect an attack from this direction. All day long the Bodies were trying to reinforce Contalmaison, but we kept them under our fire and inflicted considerable casualties. At one time two Red Cross motor vans came up to Contalmaison; and our fury may be imagined when we saw the Germans, instead of loading up with wounded, unloading machine guns; but we were by now used to German methods, and nothing they could do would in any way surprise us. On this day (July 10th) our artillery bombarded Contalmaison and Quadrangle Trench with great effect, so much so that the enemy were driven out of Quadrangle Trench, where they immediately came under our fire, and we disposed of at least forty Germans by our rifle and machine gun fire as they bolted.

The attack advanced in fine style from the west under a well-timed barrage and the covering fire of our brigade from its previously captured positions.

Wave after wave went steadily through our lines with only slight casualties, and after advancing across the valley in quick time they rushed Quadrangle Trench and disappeared into the village, which, after some stiff hand-to-hand fighting, was completely secured.

Thus the two brigades of the New Army had succeeded in capturing the whoic of the objective allotted to the division, and the great Somme advance had taken a big step forward.

On July 11th we handed over under heavy shell fire and marched back to Albert, which was being shelled as we entered our billets.

My head-quarters at Albert were in a cafe which had, in less strenuous times, been occupied, I believe, as an officers' club; but it was in rather dangerous propinquity to the railway station, which was being much used at this time; and although we had a comfortable mess and bedrooms, we soon found that the place was " unhealthy." On July 12th three high explosive shells burst within a hundreds yards of our house, and since the walls were very thin I decided that we should move on, and gave orders for everything to be packed up and clear in one hour. A further shell in the stable yard added to our agility, and immediately afterwards our horses went clattering out of the gates, and we all took our departure.

We had only vacated this charming furnished residence for half an hour before a shell got it fair and square, and most of the interior was wrecked.

We had a more peaceful time in another house, but the enemy continued to shell Albert, and what with the constant expectation of incoming shells and the incessant din of our heavies, our rest was hardly as complete as we could wish, and even so was suddenly cut short.

On July 15th we were informed that the

Division had lost heavily, and that as we had suffered least of our division, we were to be lent to the former, which was now in the line. It is always rather upsetting when you have been through a living hell, and are expecting to go right back to rest, suddenly to have to " bout turn " and re-enter the dust and the din; but it is particularly vexatious when you are lent away from your own folk. But there it isâ C est la guerre! and we marched eastward again along the Albert-Bapaumc Road to the Usna-Tara line of trenches. Now numerous heavies had been brought up just in rear of this line, and the noise was most fatiguing to men who were already feeling the strain which they had endured for fifteen days.

On July 15th I went up to reconnoitre our new line, which we were ordered to take over the next day, and I looked down from

Bailiff Wood straight along what was practically a continuation of the valley which we took by Contalmaison. There, at the end of this curving valley, I saw Pozieres, and was struck by the extraordinary fine defensive position it made, dominating the whole of the approach up twelve hundred yards of valley which gently rose to the village of Pozieres itself. Away to my right, where a division had been attacking, the old German second trench system was on high ground on the right side of the valley, and this appeared to be the most likely approach to Pozieres.

On the night of July 16th, our brigade relieved the X and Y Brigades of the

Division, both of which had been badly cut up in previous attacks. Here the supports held the Bailiff Wood hne which we had captured a few days before.

The front line which we took over from one of the relieved brigades was nothing but a few holes, and afforded very bad shelter, and the whole of our system was kept under a continual shell fire of by far the fiercest description we had yet encountered on the Somme, whilst there was no communication trench dug forward from Bailiff Wood to the new line.

During the night we set to work to dig, and the Durhams managed to dig forward as far as two small spinneys on our left, and also three considerable sections of front trench were dug, although it was impossible that night to join up.

Now I had been instructed to make a frontal attack on Pozieres on the morning of the 18th up the valley, but I asked leave first to attempt to capture a continuous trench which was between my line and Pozieres, because it seemed to me that, if that trench was strongly held with machine guns, there was little chance of any attack being able to carry right through and capture the large village behind with my very tired brigade. My request was acceded to, and the D. L. I, were ordered to attack this trench on the night of July 17th at 8 p. m.

The artillery plan was a heavy bombardment for some time previous, and a sudden barrage fire by divisional artillery at 8 p. m., under which the D. L. I, were to advance. Something went Avrong however. By the time the whole of the attackers were launched at 8.4 p. m., an intense machine gun fire was opened on the advancing infantry.

A few men only of the Durhams succeeded in reaching the enemy trench, and these were either killed or captured, the supporting waves being absolutely stopped by the fire of machine guns, estimated to be at least ten in number. Under this fire one company on the left lost every officer.

Most of the front wave succeeded in getting within forty or fifty yards of the enemy's trench, but then cross machine gun fire and wire prevented farther progress; and after dark the survivors came back after staying about an hour in No Man's Land under heavy fire.

All the wounded were brought in that night.

In view of the main attack on the village at dawn, which was still on the cards, three battalions prepared to attack; but the German trench was full of fighting troops and machine guns and apparently unaffected by our artillery; and my own view on the spot was that if the attack went on without further preparation I should not achieve my object, and my brigade would suffer very heavily. I therefore gave this view to the higher authorities, and was greatly relieved at about midnight to receive an order that the operation was cancelled.

We now set to work to try and dig a complete fire trench and j umping-off trench; and on the days and nights of the 18th and 19th we consohdated about 1,600 yards of new trench in front, and not only included the two little spinneys on the left in our line, but gained contact with the brigades on our right and left, where previously there were gaps of several hundred yards. We also dug forward in one place to within forty yards of the centre of the German trench, where we established and fortified a post after a short fight.

This complete new system, which we dug within 250 yards of the enemy, greatly assisted the Australians in their combined and successful attack on Poziercs on a later date.

My head-quarters were in the " Sausage Valley," in a deep and very stuffy German dugout, and we Avere subjected to a good deal of shelling by day and gas shelling, particularly, by night.

Carrying parties had a very bad time, and any one going from Brigade Headquarters up to the line had a particularly lively hour's march, especially in the neighbourhood of Bailiff Wood, where the enemy was throwing heavy shells with lavish hand.

On July 19th we were very glad to hear that an Australian Division was coming CH. x THE COMING OF THE ANZACS 225 up to relieve us; but this day was most unpleasant, as the front system and the Sausage Valley were shelled all day long; and from 5 p. m. the enemy poured gas shells into the Sausage Valley, so that all the gas drifted down to the lowest ground where my dugout was situated, and by which a whole Australian Brigade had to come.

In Brigade Head-quarters our eyes were streaming for at least seven hours, and the gas was more unpleasant than the usual tear shells, with the result that we had to keep our helmets on the whole time, and the relieving brigade of the â Australian

Division had the very unpleasant and difficult task of marching up on relief in the dark, in their gas helmets. The relief, notwithstanding, was admirably carried out, and rarely had we known greater efficiency in any relief than that by the Anzacs on this occasion.

During these days of fighting in unorganised territory, where frequently posts are thrown out some way in front or to flanks, the relief is rarely quite complete till dawn, and on this occasion I got away from the Sausage Valley at about 3 a. m., and after many hours of a gas mask it was delightful to go back in the cool of the early morning to rest.

I remember as we neared Becourt Wood, where my chargers were waiting, we saw a fine-looking Anzac on his horse, silhouetted against the rising sun, when he dropped his baccy pouch by accident, and the next moment he had slipped right round his seventeen-hand horse's belly, picked his pouch off the ground, and recovered his seat â a fine effort; but really, at 3 a. m., a little exacting.

Now we are in the saddle and trotting by the field guns as they herald the new day with hideous din, and on we clatter into Albert while a shell whistles over our heads and bursts a quai'ter of a mile ahead. When we reached the spot two huddled shapes lie across the road never to move again. But we are very tired, and there comes a time when fatigue makes your senses dull even to death and the shells which are his messengers. So at last to bed and sleep.

The brigade reached Albert at 4 a. m. on July 20th, and the same day we marched back ten miles to rejoin our division, which had been resting a week in the neighbourhood of Franvillers.

At this place we were glad to receive drafts for the brigade, and so we began to reorganise. Here we were inspected by the commander of the Corps, who spoke to the brigade and warmly thanked all ranks for the part they had played in the two series of operations in which tliey had taken such a strenuous part.

Whilst here also, the funeral took place at a village near by of Major-General Ingou-ville Williams, a very gallant gentleman, who never seemed happy unless he was sharing the risks of the heaviest bombardment with his men.

The ceremony was very impressive, and a distinguished company was gathered to pay a last tribute, whilst the pipes moaned and sobbed their parting chant to a warrior who did not know the meaning of fear.

Our rest was, alas, far too shortâ only five daysâ and no one had had time to recover before we were moving again to the sound of the guns, and on July 26th we marched from Franvillers right up to Contalmaison and relieved another Infantry brigade in the old German trenches north-east of that village.

In these trenches, which were in a very poor state, we joined the right of the Australian Division, and the dividing line was what was known as Munster Alleyâ a trench held by the enemy which ran at right angles from our front trench straight into the enemy's switch line.

Now, Munster Alley was the scene of very heavy fighting, and bomb fights had swayed to and fro up this trench and back. A British division had attacked up Munster Alley, and so had the Australians, and when we arrived the latter were having another effort, and after advancing about fifty yards and having a very stiff fight, had been compelled to fall back again to their starting point.

This was the state of affairs when I took over the line and was also ordered to relieve the Australians in Munster Alley. The bomb fight, however, was so intense that the Australians were unable to vacate the trench until the morning of the 26th; but we managed to assist them, and helped to bring up bombs, etc.

â â â â â â â denotes final line captured and consolidated by the Brigade. A is the point where the brigade joined the Australian 1st Division. B is the farthest polat in Munster Alley captured by the Dnrhams. 0 is the farthest point in Munster AUey captured by the Australians. D is the work where the N. F. commanded the slopes towards Martlnpuich. O. G. I and 0.0.2 are the old German 1st and 3nd lines which the brigade occupied on going into this sector.

On the 27th we decided to try our hand on Munster Alley, and the D. L. I., after a hard bomb fight, managed to gain seventy yards and block the trench. We were heavily shelled all day in the old German system, and so we set to work at night to dig forward and deepen a ditch which went by the name of Lanes Trench, and we dug this trench, which bent forward on om right, to within fifty yards of the German switch hne.

On the next night we had further fighting in Munster Alley, but without any change in the position.

We made great friends with the Australians, and one story perhaps may not be out of place to show the spirit of these lads from under the Southern Cross.

I was walking along our trench when I discovered an Australian sitting there with a bandaged hand. I asked him what he was doing. Oh, he replied, "I am resting from our bomb fight in the Alley." I then suggested that as he was wounded he had better go back to the dressing station and rest there, at which he replied that he was presently going back to the bomb fight. I told him that he was no good there with a damaged right hand, whereat he assured me he was left-handed. I then told him to remove his bandage, and found he had two fingers blown off by a bomb; so I then ordered him to go sick and shook his left hand. He was a brave man, but I fear that although I saw him " off the premises " he may have returned to the bomb fight by a circuitous route.

On the night of the 28th we were reheved, and marched back two battahons to the Sausage Valley and two to Albert, which we reached in the early hours of the morning.

On July 31st, we had a very jolly musical evening in a delightful house in Albert. A padre was there, and proved himself no mean performer on the piano, and one of the Durhams, who has charmed many a great audience at home before the war called him, delighted us with song. The two most cheery members of the mess were Captain Hurd-Wood, the Staff captain, who had been with the brigade since its birth, and the interpreter Lieut, de Mandiarges, a handsome, cultured Frenchman, who was very dear to us all.

To-night we are all happy like boys in an English barrack mess; to-morrow, half an hour after the brigade had left again for the line, a heavy shell, guided by the hand of fate, entered their room; the Staff captain is killed, de Mandiarges is carried off mortally wounded to live only long enough to receive the Croix de Guerre, whilst two other officers, Major Botham of the Fiisihers and a young subaltern recently out from England who had been left behind to rest, were in that fatal house, and they too died in that moment for their country.

This time the brigade was divided, two battalions being lent to another brigade. The N. F. and the D. L. I, went into the line on our front and two battalions of another brigade were lent me as reserves.

During the night of August 4th a company of the N. F. on the extreme right pushed a post forward to within a few yards of the switch line, and from here, looking down on Martinpuich, dominated the German approach to the switch line. During this day and the next they inflicted with picked marksmen considerable losses on the enemy, which losses were estimated at well over a hundred, whilst our machine guns accounted for another thirty. Here an unusual incident took place, the Germans coming out with a big Red Cross flag, and we allowed them all day to gather and carry in their wounded.

I was very glad to have this opportunity of returning to civilised warfare; but how hopeless was this desire will be related later, for next morning the Germans once more reciprocated by adopting tactics to which no savage warrior of the past would ever descend.

All that day our heavies bombarded the enemy switch line in front of us and the Australians.

I decided to attack Munster Alley simultaneously with a bombing attack from our junction with the Anzacs, going north-east, and another attack over the top from our new jumping-off trenches by the loop in Butter-worth Trench, attacking north-west. Some three hours before the attack I relieved the N. F., holding the jumping-off trenches, by the D. L. I.; but unfortunately, after the relief was complete, these trenches were very heavily shelled, being almost entirely obliterated in parts; and as this shelling went on until the hour for attack, the attacking company was badly shaken when the hour arrived.

The attack commenced, and the company advanced from the loop trench and nearly reached their objective under our barrage, when a heavy fire was opened from a German trench, which, not having been bombarded, was full of Germans. To add to the confusion all the smoke and dust of the Australian bombardment drifted back on the Durhams, who could not see their officers and found themselves under a heavy machine gun and bomb fire. Captain Austen, the gallant company commander, pressed on with the few men round him and reached the German trench, and was never seen again, whilst the subaltern on his flank was hit, and the front wave wavered and began to retire.

The supporting platoons, advancing into the dust and under heavy fire, seeing the front waves retiring, and not knowing the commander was killed, thought a retirement was ordered, and returned to their trenches, when, if there had been an officer on the spot to control the situation, they must have gained their objective.

Meanwhile the bomb attack of the other company forged ahead and gained seventy yards, killing numerous Germans and succeeding in blocking the trench where they had gained ground nearly up to the point of their objective, after an exceedingly bloody and brilliant attack. Simultaneously the Australians had swept on and taken the windmill, and even penetrated beyond.

We tried to organise another attack that night to gain the rest of the objective, but our trenches were so damaged by the shelhng above referred to, and so blocked by casualties, that I had to abandon the attempt.

Before light I went up to the line to find out the exact situation, and I reached it at dawn, proceeding to Munster Alley, where the Durhams had advanced. Here I discovered that the Germans were perpetrating their most dastardly crime, bombing our wounded where they lay around the trench we had assaulted the previous evening. When it is remembered that all the previous day we had allowed them to carry in their wounded, the rage of our men can be imagined, and I am glad to say they succeeded in shooting several enemy bombers who exposed themselves in their wicked work.

Captain Clarke of the Durhams, who had previously won the Military Cross and who had been fighting all night, showed me the ground Avhcrc the attack had taken place, and then I went up to the farthest point reached with Lieut. Kaye-Butterworth, also of the Durhams. The trench was very low and broken, and he kept on urging me to keep low down. I had only reached the Battalion Head-quarters on my return when

I heard poor Butterworth, a brilliant musician in times of peace, and an equally brilliant soldier in times of stress, was shot dead by a bullet through the head. So he who had been so thoughtful for my safety had suffered the fate he had warned me against only a minute before.

It was now getting quite light, and as I looked towards the distant windmill, now only a mass of stones, I saw a considerable number of men coming over the rise from towards Martinpuich. I thought it must be a counter-attack, and turned to a gunner by my side, who lent me his glasses. There, sure enough, were the grey uniforms of Germans; but now most of the figures halted, lay down and faced the enemy, apparently firing, and then I realised by their slouch hats that this was the return of an Australian " hunting expedition," and that they were bringing back several German prisoners, whom they must have extracted from positions far past their objective.

A little later in the day, the Germans made a small counter-attack against the new Durham position. Now this was precisely what the Durhams wanted, as they were anxious to kill Germans; but although it was no affair of theirs, numerous Australians jumped out of their trenches and proceeded to charge towards the Germans, who by that time were easily repulsed by our fire.

There is no doubt that the Anzac is keen, for this was after all-night fighting!

That night we were relieved, and now at last, after thirty-five days' fighting or being shelled, during which time we had only had five days' rest behind our guns, we marched, on August 8th, away from these bloody scenes and stayed at amazingly peaceful villages in the rearâ in another world, where the eternal drab is replaced by the green of an innocent countryside.

I CANNOT leave my disjointed attempt to give my impressions of my sojourn amongst our fighters without some small but very inadequate tribute to the spirit of our great Army.

For sixteen months as a regimental officer and six as a brigade commander, I have lived amongst officers, non-commissioned officers, and men in the strange life which is limited for such long periods by earth walls. I have received, given, and seen carried out the orders to advance; I have known the crowded incidents of digging, for dear life, a newly captured line within two hundred yards of the Germans; I have waited for the dawn which will deluge you in a rain of tons of terrible metal accompanied by its tornado of sound; I have crouched for long hours whilst the mad dance of death swirls round you, front and behind, to right and left, when you pray for the night. Hundreds of hours I have spent in the trenches, seeing and wondering at that great-hearted gentleman the British soldier, and so I may claim to speak from knowledge of what things are there at the heart of things.

Never have I seen a single incident of a fit man in the great Army which has lessened my faith in my countrymen or caused me to feel shame for the flag of our race.

I have seen men, it is true, with nerves shattered and trembling like children, unable to go on facing the fight, but in those cases I know that they have been put to a greater test than mortal man is meant to bear, and that the man who is seriously concussed by shell-shock is as truly out of action as the man who has a bullet through his chest.

The fortitude of our wounded is the wonder of all who have seen, and it is only beaten by the manner of those who lie down to die.

The selfishness of the old world is left far behind, and soldier shares with soldier all the small things which make life bearable, and often a tired man will oiler to carry the rifle or kit of a comrade to prevent him falling out on the march.

CH. xiii THE SPIRIT OF THE RACE 241

I remember a division which had been fighting with heavy losses being ordered up again unexpectedly on the Somme, and the day they went into action the average sickness fell from two or three hundred to one man sick. What finer evidence could we require to prove the honour of those 20,000 men?

Who has watched a battalion march to the line and has not noticed the delightful humour which runs through all ranks, and who has seen the line of bayonets ready to jump the parapet and has not realised how much of the God there is in every man?

What company commander is there who has had to ask in vain for volunteers to go out in the night and gather in wounded from No Man's Land? Indeed, what commander is there who has not had difficulty in cutting down the number of volunteers when the lives of comrades are at stake?

War may be a hateful thing, but only the luckless who are strangers to its meaning can deny its ennobling influence, provided the cause is righteous, or that, in spite of all the devastating horrors, all the sorrows and tears, the world will be enriched by the return of the survivors of our wonderful Army.

Yes, comrades of mine, you have marched down a long, long road, but you have this consolation, that you have never faltered. You may swear and grumble at times, but that does not belittle the fact that in the greatest cause for which man ever gave himself, you have with a song and a joke faced such things as man never previously dreamed of.

Hundreds, thousands, scores of thousands, of our mates have left you to go far West, and at times we feel almost overwhelmed with grief; but should we mourn too much for them, for, whatever their lives may have been, have they not absolutely made good, and is not the way of their goingâ those young, brave ladsâ such that they have succeeded in solving the greatest mystery which faces the frail creatures of this earth: have they not renewed the hope of mankind in giving their lives for their friends?

For you who return, there is a great trust, for as you have saved, so shall you build; you at least have no " Craven fear of being great "; and, with those fine brothers of ours who have come from the far places of the earth to stand by your side in the line, you will set out to make these Islands and the outer Empire a greater, happier place.

and so the faith which called you in the hour of decision will give you power to enrich the world by consummating the union of the battlefield and the grave in the lasting union of the British brotherhood.

PRINTED BT HAZELI, WATSON AND VINT5T, LD., LONDON AND ATLES-BUUr, ENGLAND.

BOOKSo"AFTER-WAR PROBLEMS

THE GREAT PROBLEMS OF BRITISH
STATESMANSHIP.

By J. ELLIS BARKER, Author of "Modern Germany,"
â ' Great and Greater Britain," etc. 10s. 6d. net

A consideration of the principal problems of foreign domeslic and economic policy with which British statcsmansliip v ill have to deal both at the Peace Congress and afterwarcs.

GERMANY'S ANNEXATIONIST AIMS.

By S. GRUMBACH. Translated, Abbreviated and
Introduced by J. Ellis Barker. 3s. 6d. net

A comprehensive statement of Germany's annexationist aims, giving the demands of the leading German rulers, statesmen, politicians, professors, generals, business men and publicists. Separate chapters deal with Germany's aims regarding Belgium, France, Russia, the British Empire, Turkey, the Far East, America, the World.

THREE CENTURIES OF TREATIES OF PEACE AND THEIR TEACHING.

By the Rt. Hon. Sir W. G. F. PHILLIMORE, Bart., D. C. L., LL. D., late Lord Justice of Appeal. 7s. 6d. net

The object of this book is to supply materials for guidance and warniuii when the terms of the future Peace come to be settled.

THE WAR AND THE NATION. A Study in
Constructive Politics.

By W. C. D. WHETHAM, F. R. S. 6s. net

This timely volume contains a critical account of some recent enquiries into national-organisation and a consideration uf the subject from a single point of view.

THE AWAKENING OF AN EMPIRE.

By ROBERT GRANT WEBSTER. 6s. net

"Ml. Webster's book is eminently sane, sound, anil well argued."â Daily Telci i aph.

THE NEW EMPIRE PARTNERSHIP: Defence,
Commerce, Policy.

By PERCY and ARCHIBALD HURD. 6s. net

"The authors of this work have chosen an excellent and business-like title for an excellent and business-like woi k. It is tresh, forcible, re. idable, excellently documented and marshalled. It suggests rather than dictates." â Ihc Spictatur.

JOHN MURRAY, Albemarle Street, LONDON, W.

BOOKS ON THE WAR

INSIDE CONSTANTINOPLE.

During the Dardanelles Expedition. A Diplomatist's Diary, April to September, 1915. By LEWIS EINSTEIN, foriner Minister Plenipotentiary, U. S. Diplomatic Service, late Special Agent at the American Embassy. 6s. net

TWENTY-TWO MONTHS UNDER FIRE.

By Brigadier-General HENRY PAGE CROFT, C. M. G., M. P. With Maps. 5s. net

The record of a Member of Parliament who joined his Territorial regiment on the outbreak of war, and took a long and continuous part in the fighting, including every one of the British offensives until the end of the Somme.

THE INDIAN CORPS IN FRANCE.

By Lt.-Col. J. W. B. MEREWETHER, C. I. E., and the Rt. Hon. Sir FREDERICK SMITH. Illustrated. 10s.6d. net

This history is dedicated by perm ssion to His Majesty the King-Emperor, and published under the authority of His Majesty's Secretary of State for India in Council.

CAPTIVITY AND ESCAPE.

By M. JEAN MARTIN. Translated from the French.

The Narrative of a French Sergeant-Major, wlio was captured in the early days of the war, was confined in German prisons and made a remarkable escape. 5s. net

By FREDERICK PALMER. WITH OUR FACES IN THE LIGHT. 2s. 6d. net

A stirring message of patriolism by a distinguished American, who hopes tliat it may explain to Britons America's spirit in this wai.

WITH THE NEW ARMY ON THE SOMME.

My Second Year of the War. 6s. net

"He knows just how to weave the personal thread into his story of great battles."â Daily Chronicle.

MY YEAR OF THE WAR. Fourth Impression. 6s. net

Including an Account of Experiences with the Troops in P'rance, and the Record of a Visit to the Grand Fleet, which is iierc given for the firs' time in its complete form.

JOHN MURRAY, Albemarle Street, LONDON, W.

By Mrs. HUMPHRY WARD 2s. 6d. nct each

TOWARDS THE GOAL

With an Introduction by Theodore Roosevelt.

Mr. Roosevelt in his Introduction. â " In this volume Mrs. Ward draws a wonderful picture of the English in the full tide of their successful effort."

Morning Post. â " A refreshing antidote to all forms of war weariness and pessimism."

The Observer. â " A worthy and high-minded successor to her ' England's Effort.""

The Globe. â " It is more interestingâ and that is a great thing to sayâ than any novel she has ever written."

4th Edition (3rd Impression)

ENGLAND'S EFFORT

With a Preface by The Earl of Rosebery, K. G.

The Times. â " Mrs. Humphry Ward has done England and the Empire a service. the cumulative effect of her plain tale is overwhelming. Facts, observed at first hand, and narrated with convincing personal touches and a nice sense of proportion."

Daily Telegraph. â " Her facts, powerfully and convincingly arrayed, leavened with humour and adorned with many human episodes, are the best antidote to depression we have yet encountered."

Bookman. â " It is an impressive record of his country's spiritual and material vitality and greatness that every Briton should be glad to possess."

JOHN MURRAY, Albemarle Street, LONDON, W.

BOOKS by BOYD CABLE

"Boyd Cable is already one of the prose Laureates of the war. No one can describe more vividly the fierce confusion of trench fighting. 'â Punch.

New and Cheaper Edition. 2s. 6d. net

BETWEEN THE LINES spectator. â " F;. r a conspectus of daily routine within the limited area of first-line trenches we think Mr. Boyd Cable's book the most fully informing we have read. If one cannot see the life of the trenches going on by reading this book, it must be that one cannot derive a true impression from any printed page."

3rd Impression. 5s. net

GRAPES OF WRATH

Westminster Gazette. â " The war has been the means of introducing to the reading stay-at-home public many powerful writers; but not one of them is quite the equal of Mr. Boyd Cable in making warfare seem real. in his new book he has surpassed his earlier accomplishments."

4th Impression. 5s. net

ACTION FRONT

Observer. â " Vivid, unforgettable sketches. No one could do more useful or desirable work tlian this of interpreting the life of the Front to tlic anxious public at home; and no one does it better than Mr. Cable."

JOHN MURRAY, Albemarle Street, LONDON, W.

Notable New Novels

HIS LAST BOW. Some Reminiscences of Sherlock Holmes

By ARTHUR CONAN DOYLE 6s. net

The friends of Mr. Sherlock Holmes will be glad to learn that he is still alive and well though somewhat crippled by occasional attacks of rheumatism. He had determined that his retirement was a permanent one, but the approach of the war caused him to lay his remarkable combination of intellectual and practical activity at the disposal of the Government, with historical results which are recounted in "His Last Bow."

UNGONQUERED. An Episode of 1914

By MAUD DIVER, Author of " Desmond's Daughter," etc.

6s. net.

Mrs. Diver tells a story of the enchantment cast upon a strong; man of high ideals by a calculating beauty, whom love of selfish ease holds back from the unquestioning sacrifices-demanded by the war,

FISHPINGLE. A Romance of the Countryside

By HORACE A. VACHELL, Author of "Quinneys'," etc.

2nd Impression. 5s, net.

"A vigorous, interesting dramatic story,. most excellent reading."â Country Life.

"A true holiday novel."â Land and Water.

HAWK OF THE DESERT

By Miss G. E. MITTON 5s. net.

The very breath of the desert is in this book; but the scenery comes second to the story, which is concerned with a knot of half a dozen people, drawn together by the threads of fate, who play out their parts in a thrilling drama.

THE WEIRD O' THE POOL

By ALEX STUART 5s, net.

A romantic story of smuggling on the Scottish coast between Bei-wick and Edinburgh at the opening of last century.

LONDON: JOHN MURRAY

Notable New Novels 5s. net each

THE LOST NAVAL PAPERS

By BENNET COPPLESTONE, Author of "Jitny and the Boys."

A series of exciting stories which reveal the Engush Secret Service as it really is; silent, unsleeping, and supremely competent.

THE BLACK OFFICE and other Chapters of Romance

By A. and E. CASTLE, Authors of "Rose of the World," etc.

Stories built of the stufif of true romance, which will carry the mind away from the anxieties of the present to the picturesque past of heroism by land and sea.

MISS MARY

By KATHARINE TYNAN, Author of " Kit," etc.

"Miss Mary" is one of Katharine Tynan's charming Irish stories, fused with that love of country which is a passion to the best of the sons and daughters of Ireland.

TRANSACTIONS OF LORD LOUIS LEWIS

Described by ROLAND PERTWEE

Diverting stories of the experiences ot a wealthy amateur collector of works of art.

"It is really very good indeed, for the author has not merely hit upon a comparatively unexplored field, but has cultivated his find with skill and a nice sense of character."â Tie Spectator

By L. ALLEN MARKER, Author of " Miss Esperance and Mr. Wycherly," etc. znd Impression.

"Of the fun and charm of small children nobody can tell a better tale than Mrs. Allen Marker. You will not easily find a book which gives more rest and refreshment."â Daily Telegraph.

LONDON: JOMN MURRAY

By HORACE A. VACHELL.

FISHPINGLE 5s. net,

An irresistibly attractive story of country life.

QUINNEYS'–Is. 3d. net and 5s. net.

A lovable story that makes real and lasting friends. Joe Quinney Is a remarkable creation, always human and intensely real.

LOOT— Is. 3d. net and 5s. net.

Each story in this book is a finely-wrought cameo of Mr. Vachell's art. Full of happy memories of wit, wisdom, and romance.

THE TRIUMPH OF TIM– 6s. net.

"A fine outstanding book. It is never dull, and the dialogue particularly is always piquant."â Pall Mall Gaxttte.

THE HILL 5s. net.

A wholesome, thoroughly manly novel, In which the author has done for Harrow what Hughes did for Rugby.

BROTHERS– 2s. 6d. net and 5s. net.

"A book to love and to live in awhile, and a book which will not Lg htly be forgotten."â Westminster Gazette,

QUINNEYS'. A Comedy in 4 Acts. Paper, Is. net; Cloth, 2s, net.

SEARCHLIGHTS. A Play in 3 Acts. Paper. Is. net; Cloth, 2s. net.

THE CASE OF LADY CUMBER. A Play in 4 Acts. Paper, Is. net; Cloth, 2s. net.

By Evelyne E. Rynd.

MRS. GREEN 2S. 6d. net. British Weekly.

'It is a delightful experience for the critic when he finds a book which he can thoroughly and heartily praise. It is a special pleasure when the book is by a new writer. In this rather undistinguished Spring season I have found no book on fiction nearly so good and promising. There are not many wittier or kindlier scribes at work among us, and very few with such a quality of freshness." World.

' A creation of genuine and well-sustained humour, the " Mrs. Green " papers should not be overlooked by any who at the present season are seeking light literature with plenty of laughter in it."

MRS. GREEN AGAIN 2s. 6d. net. Morning Post.

'it is, perhaps, only necessary to say of " Mrs. Green Again " that Miss Evelyne Rynd's new book is "up to sample," and that the now well-known creature of her fancy and observation is as full of humorous perversities and whimsicalwisdom as ever. For Mrs. Green, the garrulous wife of " little " Green, the gardener at a country parsonage, is, or ought to be, familiar in every household that cherishes the traditions of English country life." Pall Mall Gazette.

' Mrs. Green is as lively, shrewd, and humorous as ever; and her circumlocuied speech, which, however, is never allowed to obscure her train of thought is managed with all Miss Rynd's accustomed def r fss.

Murray's 13 Novels

MICHAEL O'HALLORAN. By Gene Stratton-Porter.

"Be Square " is Micky's slogan. To read this refreshing story Is a tonic. It is full of the joy of life.

LADDIE. By Gene Stratton-Porter.

"Laddie" strikes straight at the heart, and brings with It all the country glamour and goodness of life In the old farmhouse where the author's girlhood was spent.

LOOT. By Horace A. Vachell.

Each story in this book is a finely-wrought cameo of Mr. Vachell's art. Full of happy memories of wit, wisdom and romance.

MR. WYCHERLY'S WARDS. By L. Allen Harker.

Continuing that delightful story " Miss Esperance and Mr. Wycherly." The glamour of youth and springtime happily contrasted with the beautiful serenity of age. A book to readâ and re-read.

TOWER OF IVORY. By Gertrude Atherton.

Joy, passion and the conflict In a woman's soul are set forth with all the fascination of Mrs, Gertrude Atherton's art. The subtle character studies bite into the memory. A more interesting or compelling story has not been written for many years.

NOTWITHSTANDING. By Mary Cholmondeley.

Crammed with wit and wisdom. Illuminated by wondrous touches and brilliant characterization. A splendid book for these times. Full of Ufe and abounding in vital human Interest.

FRECKLES. By Gene Stratton-Porter.

Considerably over one million copies of this delightful Novel have been sold.

OUINNEYS'. By Horace A. Vachell.

A lovable story that makes real and lasting friends. Joe Quinney Is a remarkable creation, always human and intensely real.

Miss ESPERANCE and Mr. WYCHERLY.

By L. Alien Harker.

SEPTIMUS. By W. J. Locke.

iuE FLORENTINE FRAME. By Elizabeth Robins.

FLEMINGTON. Bv Violet Jacob.

OTHER STORIES BY MRS. L. ALLEN MARKER.

THE FFOLLIOTS OF REDMARLEY 5s. net.

"I have just returned from a delightful week-end. The hoise, called Redmarley, is a charming old place, situate, as the auctioneers say, in one of the most picturesque neighbourhoods in the Cotswolds; so there was plenty of good scenery. But my friends with whom I was staying would make any spot happy. Ffouiot is the name of them, and they are the jolhest, most companionable folk in the world. Perhaps Mr. Ffouiot (who has nerves, reads Walter Pater and doesn't appreciate noise) might be a little bit in the way; but, as he hardly ever leaves his study, that need worry nobody. Mrs. Ffouiot is an angelâ so pretty and unselfish and sympathetic that it is no wonder that her crew of deughtful children simply adore her. I wish I had time to tell you more about the children. Two of them are practically grown up; indeed Mary astonished us all, at the end of my visit, by becoming engaged to a nice soldier (just when I myself was almost sure she would marry the young Radical M. P. who so admired herâ but it was better as things happened). The others will miss her awfully when she goes to India. Still, the house can hardly be dull, as there are two delightful infants growing up; and meanwhile there are the Rugby twins, Uz and Buz, to keep things lively. We had great fun one evening when Buz dressed up as a Suffragette and interviewed young Mr. Gallup about votes for womenâ and I must say the latter took the joke very well. But then everybody in or near Redmarley is like that. Would you care to meet them all for yourself? Then buy Mrs. L. Allen Harker's new book. It is called quite simply. The Ffolliots of Redmarley (John Murray, 5s.), and I pity you if you don't end by regarding every character in it as a personal friend."â Punch.

"Oh yes, you can't help liking it. And how cleverly Mrs. L. Allen Harker can paint youth 1 The young people among whom her new story. The Ffolliots of Redmarley, is written are perfectly fascinating and so real. You can't help loving them; their breeziness is so healthy and exhilarating."â The Taller.

BY MRS. L. ALLEN HARKER.

MR. WYCHERLY'S WARDS

Is. net. and 5s. net.

"The book so absolutely charmed me that the moment I had finished it I turned back to the first page and read it through again. I shall read it a third time very soon."â Truth.

"Then Jane Anne, one of the most fascinating child-creations in modern fiction, comes on the scene. Jane Anne is everything by turn and nothing long, but always fascinating, natural, and interesting. she will delight those who now make her acquaintance, and once to have known Jane Anne is to have her ever in remembrance. Many delicate touches illumine these pages, wherein, too, is much quiet humour, and few will lay aside the book, we fancy, without feeling that they would like to have been a visitor at that house in Holywell."â The World.

"There are very few writers who have as much to offer us in the way of distinctive charm as Mrs. Allen Harker. Her new book is a continuation of that delightful work. Miss Esperance and Mr. Wycherly. Miss Esperance is dead, and Mr. Wycherly is left guardian to those fascinating boys Edmund and Montagu. But more fascinating than the boys is the other ward that Mr. Wycherly adopts, by name Jane Anne. We can only hope that Mrs. Harker is going to continue her study of the career of Jane Anne."â Morning Post.

"We have to thank Mrs. Harker for a charming and tender comedy of Youth and Age."â The Spectator.

"Brilliant piece of work, full of delicate humour, clever character-drawing, and no little of unforced and tender pathos. Little Jane Anne is a finely conceived character, and shows us Mrs. Harker at her very best. Not many books nowadays possess the originality and charm of freshness which characterize this author's dehghtful work. It is a thoroughly enjoyable and thoroughly artistic piece of work, and is to be cordially recommended."â Liverpool Daily Post.

BY MRS. L. ALLEN MARKER.

MISS ESPERANCE MR. WYCHERLY

Is. net. and 5s. net.

"If you want to give yourself a delightful treat get Miss Esperance and Mr. Wycherly and enjoy every word of it. The book so absolutely charmed me that the moment I had finished it I turned back to the first page and read it through again. I shall read it a third time very soon."â Truth.

"Having given the necessary time for the critical spirit to get even with emotion, we may say that it is long since we have read a book so full of tenderness, humanity, and charm. It should take very high rank indeed, and pass into the list of those books which are not disposed of when the year is over. The book is pure gold."â Daily Telegraph.

"The most dehghtful book of its kind we have ever read. A story of the Cranford type, as gracefully written, as full of tender humour as Mrs. Gaskell's masterpiece, and even more endearing. It is impossible within a few lines to give any impression of such a book as this, nor is it really necessary, for every one who is capable of appreciating true literature will read it with sympathetic tears and laughter, and return to it lovingly as one meets and greets tried and faithful friends."â Lady.

"A book like this is a pure delight, so genuine is the laughter it evokes, so untouched by anything of a maudlin nature is the delicate sentiment it mingles with the mirth. They will be queer-minded people, either young or old, who cannot appreciate this book."â Daily Chronicle.

"This is the most charming and tender child-story that has appeared for a very long time. We have read this book with the greatest pleasure, and hope it will find its way into many a home."â Christian World.

Lightning Source UK Ltd.
Milton Keynes UK
UKOW051530120312

188825UK00003B/226/P